Self-Publish Your Books on Kindle and Promote them to Bestseller Status

STRATEGIC POSITIONING
P R E S S

Oxford and London

CRUSH IT WITH KINDLE

John Tighe

www.CrushItwithKindle.com

Published by Strategic Positioning Press Limited
Printed by CreateSpace, Charleston SC
2nd edition
First published in 2012
This edition first published in 2014

ISBN-10: 0990470202

ISBN-13: 978-0-9904702-0-5

Strategic Positioning Press Limited
White Barn
Manor Farm
Wantage
Oxon, OX12 8NE
United Kingdom

Praise for Crush It with Kindle

"Promoting books on Kindle creates a different set of challenges to those you face when marketing a physical book. John guides you expertly through these challenges and makes the process clear and easy to understand."

Marci Shimoff — NY Times Bestselling Author of *Happy for No Reason: 7 Steps to Being Happy from the Inside Out* and *Chicken Soup for the Woman's Soul*

"I love the 80/20 Principle approach that John takes to successfully marketing Kindle books. As he explains, there are thousands of things you could do to promote your book, but most of your results will come from just a handful – and John has identified the ones that will make the biggest difference."

Chris Attwood — Co-author of the NY Times Bestseller, *The Passion Test: The Effortless Path to Discovering Your Life Purpose*

"Crush It with Kindle is a great resource guide for anyone wanting to publish and promote their books on Kindle the right way. It's a book that you'll want to refer back to again and again."

Janet Bray Attwood — Co-author of the NY Times Bestseller, *The Passion Test: The Effortless Path to Discovering Your Life Purpose*

"John has a great way of taking complex things and simplifying them so that they're easy to follow, step-by-step and highly actionable. If you're planning to write a Kindle book then Crush It with Kindle is a must read."

Geoff Affleck — Co-author of the #1 bestselling eBook, *Enlightened Bestseller: 7 Keys to Creating a Successful Self-Help Book*

About the Author

JOHN TIGHE is an online marketing expert, entrepreneur, bestselling author, speaker, business coach and founder and CEO of the Strategic Positioning Press publishing house.

Before striking out on his own John had a career as a corporate lawyer, but decided he wanted more from life. Today, instead of being chained to his desk at a law firm, John works with authors and entrepreneurs from around the world helping them to successfully write, publish and promote their books.

John's primary focus, through the Strategic Positioning Press, is helping experts and entrepreneurs in a wide range of fields to strategically position themselves by becoming bestselling published authors. This positioning allows them to rapidly grow their businesses by attracting more of their ideal clients and by being able to charge higher fees.

This book is dedicated to my
mother, my father and my brother.

Thank you for a lifetime of support
and encouragement without which
I could not be where I am today.

"I challenge you to make your life a masterpiece.
I challenge you to join the ranks of those people
who live what they teach, who walk their talk"

—Tony Robbins

"It is not the critic who counts; not the man who points out how
the strong man stumbles, or where the doer of deeds could have
done them better.

"The credit belongs to the man who is actually in the arena, whose
face is marred by dust and sweat and blood; who strives valiantly;
who errs, who comes short again and again, because there is no
effort without error and shortcoming; but who does actually strive
to do the deeds; who knows great enthusiasms, the great devotions;
who spends himself in a worthy cause; who at the best knows in the
end the triumph of high achievement, and who at the worst, if he
fails, at least fails while daring greatly, so that his place shall never be
with those cold and timid souls who neither know victory nor
defeat."

—Theodore Roosevelt

Contents

Preface to 2014 edition

This book was first published in December 2012. Since then Amazon have made some big changes that need to be taken into account when you promote your books and this edition has been updated to reflect them.

I've also added two brand two new chapters. The first of these explains how to format your book – something that I found a lot of people were getting stuck on. The second takes you step-by-step through the process of publishing your book to Amazon via the KDP (Kindle Direct Publishing) platform.

Meanwhile, the original chapter covering how to market your books has been updated and greatly expanded to the point that the material now covers four distinct chapters.

These updates and additions are all good reasons for bringing out a revised and updated 2014 edition.

There is another reason, however. When I clicked the "Save and Publish" button back in December 2012 I had no idea how successful the book would be or what it would lead to:

Since then I've had the privilege of speaking about Kindle publishing on stage and to author groups around the world as well as giving numerous interviews on the subject.

I've also been involved in the publication and promotion of many more books since then (some my own, some on behalf of clients) with each promotion being a chance to test new ideas and see what's working best *now*.

Additionally, I now teach a course on Kindle publishing, which allows me to interact with students in both group and one-on-one coaching sessions, answer their questions and find out where their sticking points are.

I bring these things up for two reasons. The first is because they allow me to write a better book for you: The 2014 edition of Crush It with Kindle benefits from all the learning and experience I've had since the book first came out and reflects all the key changes made by Amazon.

The second reason I bring them up is to drive home the point that you never know where your book will take you until you publish it. I've had some amazing experiences and met many wonderful people since publishing Crush It with Kindle – none of which would have happened if I hadn't made the time to write, publish and promote the book.

It is my sincere hope that your publishing journey will lead to amazing experiences for you too. Not the least of which, of course, is the pride at becoming a published author – and, all going to plan, a bestselling published author. Whatever your publishing hopes and dreams may be this book is designed to help you get there as quickly and efficiently as possible.

Good luck on your journey!

John Tighe

Oxford, England, 27th April 2014

Who is this book for?

Have you ever dreamt about becoming a published author? Do you have "a book inside you" or a message that you want to get out to the world? Can you help solve people's problems with your knowledge? Is there a novel you long to write? Are you an entrepreneur or business owner who would like to position yourself as an expert and win more business?

Is the answer to any of these questions is "Yes" then this book is for you.

There are many valid reasons for wanting to write a book. For some authors the primary motivation is their love of writing; for others the motivation is more commercial, for example, a book is a great way to generate business. Whatever your personal reasons may be they are entirely valid as long as you follow this one golden rule:

Your books must provide value for your readers.

That value may come in the form of knowledge or entertainment or both, but it must be there. If it's not then your book has little chance of success and, frankly, you've got to ask whether a book that doesn't provide value is worth writing in the first place!

The reason I'm saying this at the start of this book is because I've seen too many books and courses on Kindle publishing that basically teach the following:

"Throw up lots of crappy little Kindle books and try and make a few dollars from each – that will make you rich."

Not only is this wrong ethically, it is also a terrible business strategy. It leads to bad reviews, poor to non-existent sales and a high refund rate. Furthermore, as time goes on Amazon will doubtless crackdown increasingly hard on poor content and rightly so – they are in the business of providing a great experience for their customers, not allowing scam artists to rip them off.

What I am saying, to put it bluntly, is that this book is not for those looking for a "get rich quick scheme".

This book is for people who want to write books that provide real value for their readers – books that they can feel genuinely proud of.

Getting into Kindle publishing

Here's where I give you, very briefly, the story of how I got into Kindle publishing and how I came to write this book.

I've always loved books and from that love of books grew a love of writing. I began work on my first book way back in 1998. It was a novel – a thriller – and I spent hours researching and writing it over several months. I loved the idea of being a writer – of getting paid to do something I loved while reaching thousands of people with my work. Unfortunately, when I tried to get an agent that vision collided with reality and all I ended up with was dozens of rejection letters. Without an agent, of course, it's virtually impossible to get your book in front of a publisher. I know there are plenty of writers out there, both published and unpublished, who can empathize with that experience.

I'll be honest and say that this experience knocked my confidence. I didn't begin writing my second book until January 2004. This was a non-fiction book on health, nutrition and weight loss (I had spent several years working as a personal trainer, fitness coach and nutrition coach before I wrote it). Again, I couldn't get an agent. The feedback was that the book was good, but because it was such a competitive market I would need a celebrity fronting the book for it to succeed. Except that, even if I could have got one, I didn't want a celebrity: it was my book – a labor of love and the culmination of years of studying and then applying what I knew with over a thousand clients!

And that was it for a long time, both manuscripts gathering digital and physical dust and all but forgotten about... until mid-2012 when I first learned about Kindle Direct Publishing.

Kindle Direct Publishing

Kindle Direct Publishing is something that, when you hear about it, sounds too good to be true.

"So, let me get this right... Amazon will allow you to publish your own book on Kindle without having an agent or a publisher. It can be published in less than 24 hours once your manuscript is ready and they will make it available to millions of Amazon users around the world and pay you 70% royalties... Wow!"

Immediately, I started investigating Kindle Direct Publishing (KDP) and finding out how it worked. I quickly realized two things – first, that maybe that work I'd done all those years ago wasn't wasted after all. Second, that I had the chance to begin writing again – only this time I could do it secure in the knowledge that I would definitely get published. Sure, I would be responsible for the initial marketing of my books, but that's pretty much the case for all first time authors anyway. Plus, I knew from studying how Amazon worked and how other authors had successfully used the KDP program that if I could reach a certain tipping point then Amazon would begin promoting my book for me.

This really fired me up! And so, just a few days after discovering Kindle Direct Publishing, I began writing my third book. Only this time I did so with a sense of confidence and calm that I'd never had before. My third book was about real estate – specifically about how to sell your house and get the best price without getting ripped off. This was something I knew a lot about because I had spent the previous four years running an online real estate company advising clients on exactly that. I felt it was an important message to get out because a lot of people get taken advantage of – often without their ever even realizing it.

When I finished the book in October 2012 I knew that the next step was to work out a marketing plan. Fortunately, because my real estate business was online I had four years' experience of online marketing – a subject that I had studied a great deal, not only to help promote the business, but because I found it fascinating in its own right. So it wasn't too much work to fill in the gaps in my knowledge that were specific to Kindle marketing and to promoting books on Amazon.

Once I'd done that I was able to set out my marketing plan step-by-step and formulate a time line for the various tasks I had to do.

The evolutionary next step I didn't think of at first – the idea took a couple of days to dawn. Then it hit me – "I could teach this!" I realized there must be thousands of frustrated authors out there (just like me a few weeks earlier) who either weren't aware of Kindle Direct Publishing or weren't sure how to use it to publish and promote their books. Having just gone through the process myself and with a background in marketing I knew could really help them. And, I could do it combining three of my great loves – writing, teaching and online marketing. That's how I ended up writing this, my fourth book, the original version of which was published in December 2012.

Why am I telling you all this. Well, first of all I think it's important that you know where I'm coming from in writing this book. I love to write and I've been through the frustration of being a rejected and unpublished author. In fact, that was part of my identity for fourteen years before I finally discovered Kindle Direct Publishing and effectively got given the "keys to the kingdom".

I'm also a marketer – in particular, an online marketer, which is highly relevant to Kindle. Since 2009 I've sold hundreds of thousands of dollars' worth of products and services online. And that, I believe, gives me a real edge when it comes to teaching you what you need to know in order not just to *publish* your books but also to *promote* them. That's important, because you might have a great book or a truly valuable message but if people don't discover it then they can't benefit from it.

Staying on the marketing theme, it's worth mentioning here that while the obvious way of making a living from your book is through royalties it's not the only way. Kindle books, because they can contain links to web pages, lend themselves to a variety of ways of generating income (covered in chapter 2). Not all of these will appeal to or be appropriate to every author. For example, if you're a writer of fiction then product sales are not an obvious fit. However, you may be able to generate additional sales by adding links to the end of each of your books in order to cross-promote your other books. You may also have success building up an email list of people who enjoy your work so that you can keep them up to date with new projects and let them know when you launch a new title.

Something else I'd like to touch on here is motivation and the idea that you don't necessarily have to write your own books. Outsourcing work to a ghostwriter is a concept that some writers struggle with. Some even go as far as to argue that unless someone is primarily motivated by a love of writing then somehow their book is less valid. Although I love writing (and I write all my own books) I have to disagree with this – just my personal view. People have lots of different reasons for publishing a book and who am I to suggest they shouldn't do so unless they've written it themselves or that if they are not the writer their book lacks validity? Some people have important messages that they're passionate about yet don't enjoy writing or simply don't have the time to do it. Others may not want to write themselves, but can help others get their work out to the world by taking on the role of publisher.

The truth is that the traditional publishing industry uses ghostwriters all the time. And it's not just publishers bringing in ghostwriters to write "autobiographies" for celebrities and politicians either. Ghostwriters often help experts get their ideas into print or help fiction authors keep up with public demand for new novels.

Like I said, I don't think there's anything wrong with ghostwriting, provided that you follow the golden rule that we talked about earlier:

Your books must provide value for your readers.

To really succeed your book needs to be well written *and* well marketed. Take either away and you will limit your success. And remember, the more value you give to your readers – whether in the form of entertainment or knowledge – the better you will do.

People have different reasons for wanting to publish on Kindle. For some it's because they love books, they love writing and they've always wanted to become a published author. For others it's because they have a message they want to get out to the world – something they're passionate about and want to teach or share. And for others, publishing on Kindle may be something they see more as a business: a way of leveraging the power of Amazon to monetize their content – or other people's.

In my case, it's a bit of all three. I've always loved books and enjoyed writing. I've definitely got ideas and information that I want to share with the world. And, yes, I'd also like to get paid and build my business while I'm doing it.

Whatever your reasons are, we're going to cover everything you need to know to become a successful and bestselling published author on Kindle.

By the way, once you become a bestselling author it's forever – it's something that you can tell people about for the rest of your life and that's pretty cool! :-)

What does this book cover?

The first step is to get your book written and then published on Kindle. Of course, it's not enough just to publish your book. You've also got to promote it – ideally to bestseller (top 100) or #1 bestseller status for one or more of its categories.

So, here's how this book is organized and what we're going to cover to get you to the point where you are a bestselling author on Amazon:

The first chapter is all about the incredible opportunity that Amazon has given us through its Kindle Direct Publishing (KDP) program. It looks at how fast eBook sales, and Kindle book sales in particular, are growing and explains why Amazon's Kindle is *the* platform to be on.

Chapter 2 looks at how you can make money through Kindle. You see, it's not just about royalties – nice as they are. There are 9 primary ways of monetizing your book, and while they may not all apply to you it's important to know what they are before you start writing so that you can plan strategically. You want to get paid for your work don't you?!

Also in chapter 2, we'll look at how you can use serialization to build a fan base, make multiple sales to people and get Amazon to cross-promote your books for you. This works for both fiction and non-fiction, though it works especially well for fiction.

In chapter 3 we'll cover how to choose your niche (if you're writing non-fiction) or genre (if you're writing fiction) so that you can maximize your sales. The last thing you want to do is write a book and find that there's no audience for it. Chapter 3 will show you how to work out the demand for a book before ever writing a single word.

Then, in chapter 4, we'll go through how to get your book written quickly – or how to outsource the writing to a ghostwriter if you don't want to do it yourself. Just to be clear, the focus of chapter 4 is on organizing your writing so that you can create your book quickly and efficiently. It is not a chapter on creative writing, which is beyond the scope of this book.

In chapter 5 we'll take a subject that causes a lot of confusion, namely, how to format your book for Kindle, and make it simple. There are many different formats to choose from. I'll show you the one I use and take you through step-by-step what to do. And if you still don't want to do it yourself I'll show you how you can outsource the entire process.

Chapter 6 shows you, step-by-step, how to publish your book on KDP once you've got your manuscript formatted and ready to go.

Chapter 7 covers what I call your book's "building a bestseller" foundations. These are the fundamentals that you must get right before even thinking about promoting your book. That's because if they're not in place you'll largely be wasting your money; on the other hand, if you get them right then everything you do to promote your book from that point on will be many times more effective.

Amazon is the 800 lb. Gorilla when it comes to eBook sales; it truly dominates the market. In chapter 8 we'll look at the benefits of getting Amazon to promote your book to a laser targeted audience of book buyers and what you have to do to make that happen.

Chapter 9 shows you how to run the perfect launch for your book – a launch that will rocket your book up the Amazon bestseller lists and get it to that vital "tipping point" where Amazon starts promoting it for you, leading to long-term success and long-term organic sales.

Finally, in chapter 10 we'll cover a range of highly effective post-launch book marketing strategies. These are the strategies that will give you the biggest bang for your buck and help keep your book in the bestseller lists and making great sales for the long-term.

Bestseller status, by the way, means getting your book in the top 100 for its category or the top 100 overall for Kindle.

Getting your book into the top 100 means you can then call yourself an Amazon bestselling author. That gives you an enormous amount of credibility and is incredibly powerful positioning.

But, what if you could do even better than that? What if could become not just a bestselling author, but a #1 bestselling author? You see while getting to #1 for all Kindle books might be a bit of a tall order, getting to #1 for your chosen category is much, much easier. The information in chapters 7, 8, 9 and 10 will show you how.

OK, almost time to get started...

Before we do, however, it's worth mentioning that things change all the time in Kindle publishing. For that reason I've set up the Crush It with Kindle Facebook page. I use it to post updates on important changes, links to new videos and Kindle marketing tips.

Before you read the rest of the book visit **Facebook.com/CrushItwithKindle** to "like" the page to keep up to date.

Chapter 1:
The Kindle publishing opportunity

So you've decided you want to get your book published and out to the world. First of all, well done!

Secondly, did you know you can now become a published author and be selling your book to Amazon's *hundreds of millions* of Kindle customers in as little as 24 hours?

That's how quickly it's possible to get your Kindle book approved by Amazon and on sale. In fact, I've seen it happen in as little as 12 hours.

And it gets better...

Kindle publishing is growing at an incredible rate and Amazon are doing everything they can to increase Kindle book sales.

Amazon has an estimated 400,000,000+ credit cards on file belonging to existing account holders. This is significant not only because of the sheer number of customers Amazon has; it has also allowed Amazon to do something incredibly clever: it has allowed them to put in place "1-Click" purchasing for Kindle books.

One-click purchasing allows Amazon account holders to buy Kindle books with just a single mouse click – no need for them to enter address or card details or to click through several pages to make a purchase. In other words, Amazon has made it <u>as easy as they possibly can</u> for their customers to buy Kindle books.

Couple this with the fact that Kindle books tend to be less expensive than physical books and "1-Click" purchasing becomes even more attractive for Amazon's customers.

Now factor in that Kindle books can be downloaded instantly. Even Amazon "Prime" members have to wait at least a day for a physical book to be shipped to them – and most Amazon customers typically wait 3 to 5 days for their books to arrive. With a Kindle book gratification is instant!

What Amazon has done by combining "1-Click" purchasing, lower price points and instant gratification is turn Kindle books into the *ultimate impulse purchase*. This is, of course, incredibly good news for us as Kindle authors – Amazon has created the perfect online ecosystem for selling the maximum number of our books.

Nor is this the only very clever thing that Amazon has done that benefits us as authors:

The Kindle app

Hundreds of millions of Kindle devices have been sold since the first Kindle was launched in November 2007. However, despite these numbers not everyone owns a Kindle. This is something that Amazon has addressed by giving away the free Kindle app to anyone who wants it.

The Kindle app allows any desktop computer, laptop computer, tablet or smart phone to be used as a Kindle reader. It works on any platform – Mac or PC, iPad or Android. It means that there are an estimated 5 billion plus Kindle ready devices in the world!

That means there are billions of people worldwide who can buy your Kindle books, of whom at least 400 million can do so with a single click.

Amazon wants content

And right now, Amazon desperately wants people to provide content that they can sell on Kindle because that is part of their strategy to dominate the multi-billion dollar eBook market.

Currently, Amazon's market share of eBook sales is around 65%. The more people that Amazon can get using its KDP platform to publish books the more chance they have of growing their market share. Because Amazon wants as many people as possible to provide content for them they've made it incredibly easy. So easy, in fact, that you can have your book published and on sale through Amazon in less than 24 hours.

Plus, because they want your content so badly Amazon will let you keep 70% of the royalties – by the way, that's up to ten times what an author would get through a traditional publisher.

Taking all this together, publishing on Kindle is an incredible opportunity:
1. It costs nothing to get started
2. There are zero overheads
3. You make 70% profit on sales
4. Amazon takes care of the backend for you
5. Amazon markets your book for you
6. And you can be selling in less than 24 hours

And there are other factors that make Amazon the perfect online environment in which to be selling your books and building your business. Let's look at some other facts about Amazon that help make Kindle publishing such an amazing opportunity:
1. Amazon is the world's biggest <u>buyer</u> search engine
2. Amazon is the biggest bookshop in the world (600 million+ Kindle books sold in 2013)
3. Amazon is the world's most *trusted* online retailer
4. Amazon has over 400,000,000+ credit cards on file: this allows "1-Click" impulse purchasing for Kindle books

5. Amazon will promote your books, putting them in front of *precisely targeted audiences* of <u>thousands of buyers</u>

To get an idea of how fast the eBook market is growing look at the chart below from PwC, one of the world's leading accounting firms. Bear in mind that this chart is for North American eBook sales only and that the rest of the world is catching up fast.

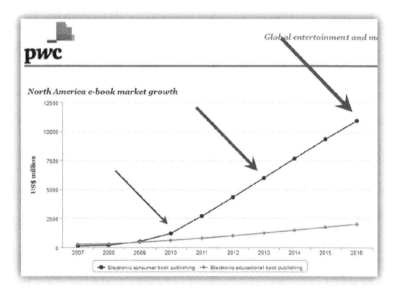

You can see that in 2010 eBook sales were worth $1.2 billion. By 2013 that number had grown to $6 billion – an increase of 500% in just three years. And by 2016 PwC estimate that eBook sales will have hit $10.9 billion and growing fast.

So, those are the numbers for eBook sales, but what about Kindle book sales specifically?

Well, if you want to get an idea of how fast Kindle book sales are growing then just take a look at this chart provided by Amazon themselves. This now famous picture was taken at Amazon's Kindle

Fire HD launch in September 2012. You will probably recognize Jeff Bezos, the founder of Amazon, making his presentation.

Physical book sales are in yellow (the line starting on the left) and are growing very strongly. However, Kindle book sales, represented by the orange line (the line on the right), are growing even faster with a growth line that's almost vertical!

Bear in mind that the first Kindle device was not released until November 2007 and initially very few people actually owned Kindles – hence the "slow" growth of Kindle book sales for the first few months (the very first Kindle app was not released until the end of 2009).

Nonetheless, Amazon was able to hit some hugely significant Kindle milestones very quickly:

- In July 2010, just 21 months after the first Kindle was launched, Kindle books outsold hardback books on Amazon for the first time.

- Then, nine months later in April 2011, Amazon sold more Kindle books than paperback and hardback combined: in other words, it took just 30 months from launch for Kindle book sales to exceed physical book sales!

- In 2013 Amazon are estimated to have sold between two and three times as many Kindle books as physical books.

The growth in Kindle book sales is not likely to stop any time soon.

The death of the gatekeeper

And, if this wasn't enough good news, the gatekeeper is no more.

You no longer have to convince an overworked agent who barely has time to glance at your manuscript that your book is worth publishing. You can now publish through Amazon as soon as your manuscript is ready and let the market decide how much they like your book.

In fact, the whole publishing landscape is changing. Authors who previously failed to find traditional publishers are now having incredible success with Kindle. Publishing houses have set up divisions whose sole function is to scout out new talent from the ranks of self-published authors.

Already we're seeing success stories like Amanda Hocking who published her first Kindle book in April 2010 because she needed to raise $300 for a trip to Chicago – to see a Muppets exhibition. She's now sold over 1.5 million eBooks and made over $2.5 million in royalties.

Now obviously Amanda is an exception. By January 2011 she was selling over 100,000 books a month.

But what if you could sell just ten books a day? Ten copies of a $4.99 book @ 70% royalties is $34.93 a day or around $1,050 a month. Those are very realistic numbers for anyone with a good book that is properly marketed. More to the point, if you've ever dreamed of becoming a full-time writer then this sort of modest success would you get you well on the way.

That's because you don't have to stop at one book – you can publish as many as you like. What if you ended up publishing five books that each sold ten copies a day for total of fifty copies? Now you're making $5,250 a month just from royalties.

(And by the way, one of the best ways to sell more books is to write more books. A person who reads and enjoys one of your books is much more likely to buy your other books than a non-reader of your work.)

Now, you have to factor in a small download charge levied by Amazon (against your royalties) for each book that you sell, but unless your book contains lots of images it's relatively small – though it does add up if you sell a lot of books. To give you an idea, the download charge every time someone buys this book is around ten cents.

With:

- Five billion plus Kindle-ready devices in the world
- Kindle book sales going through the roof
- Amazon holding 400,000,000+ credit cards on file
- "1-Click" purchasing for Kindle books, and
- Digital book sales set to hit $7.5 billion this year in North America alone and rising fast...

I hope I've convinced you how important Kindle is and what an incredible opportunity you have right now to start publishing your books on Kindle.

This book is designed to show you just how easy it is to do that. Over the next few chapters I will take you step-by-step through exactly how to write, publish and promote your books successfully on Kindle.

BONUS:
Free Crush It with Kindle video series

This book is accompanied by a free video series.

The videos feature additional bonus material that is better suited to video format. They also build on some of the key things covered in the book so watching them will allow you to get as much as you possibly can from the book.

To get instant access to the videos go to **bit.ly/ciwkvideos**

Amongst other things, the video series includes additional information on:
- Maximizing your Kindle royalties
- The 6 steps to a Kindle bestseller
- The incredible explosive growth of Kindle publishing
- Case studies and success stories

To get your bonus videos go to **bit.ly/ciwkvideos**

Chapter 2:
The 9 ways to monetize Kindle books

Apart from wanting to be a published author and getting your message out to the world, both of which are great reasons, you'll also want to get paid for your books. I said I would teach you 9 ways of monetizing your Kindle book and here they are:

1. Royalties
2. Expert positioning
3. "Commission" publishing
4. "Content" publishing
5. "Traditional" publishing
6. Product/affiliate sales
7. List building
8. Bulk buy
9. Serialization

Most of these methods apply to both fiction and non-fiction books, while a couple are more applicable for non-fiction books – I'll explain which is which as we go through.

What's important, however, is that you know about these monetization methods up front so that you can decide which ones are right for you. And, just as importantly, remember that you can monetize each of your books in multiple ways.

1. Royalties

This is the most obvious way to make money on Kindle. Don't forget, Amazon will give you 70% royalties on your book and there are no overheads! This is huge – it's up to ten times what an author would get through a traditional publisher.

In fact, a number of high profile authors have decided to leave their traditional publishers behind as they simply can't compete with self-publishing when it comes to royalties.

A recent high-profile example is Pulitzer Prize-winning author David Mamet who in 2013 decided to self-publish his latest works – a novella and two short stories. Interestingly, in a New York Times interview, one of the reasons he gave for self-publishing was that "publishing is like Hollywood — nobody ever does the marketing they promise."

In other words, not only do you get much higher royalties as a self-published author you can also (with the exception of the very top authors with big budgets behind them) do a better job of marketing your book if you do it yourself rather than leaving it to a reluctant publisher!

Amazon does have some restrictions if you want to get 70% royalties. Your book must be priced at between $2.99 and $9.99 or the local currency equivalent. Outside of this price bracket the royalties drop to 35% (which is still very good compared to traditional publishing).

This price "restriction" shouldn't really be a problem in most cases, however, because the chances are that your optimum (from a royalty point of view) price is going to sit somewhere in the $2.99 to $9.99 bracket anyway. Of course, you may want a higher book price as part of a positioning strategy or a lower book price as part of a backend strategy (more on both of these strategies below) in which case, as I said, a 35% royalty is still very good.

Maximizing your royalties

The pricing sweet spot for self-published books tends to be around $2.99. This gets you into the 70% royalty bracket, while still keeping your price low enough for your book to be an impulse purchase for many people.

However, the only way to be certain that you have priced your book for maximum royalties is to test and track your sales at different price points. All the information you need to track your sales can be found within the reports section of your KDP account.

For more information on price testing and how to calculate the royalty sweet spot for your books watch the free Crush It with Kindle video series that accompanies this book. For instant access to the video series go to bit.ly/ciwkvideos

Now making money from royalties could be your main reason for publishing on Kindle or it could be just a bonus if you end up focusing on one of the other monetization methods covered in this chapter.

There are already several Kindle millionaires so royalties can definitely be a pretty good reason in their own right! We've already looked at Amanda Hocking and how she's sold over 1.5 million eBooks and made over $2.5 million in royalties since she first published on Kindle in 2010.

Let's be honest, however, you don't have to make a million in royalties to get to a point where you can consider yourself a successful author. Most people would consider themselves very successful if they could make a few thousand dollars a month in royalties – basically, enough to live comfortably and continue to write for a living.

To put financial success into perspective, Nobel Prize-winning behavioral economist Daniel Kahneman discovered that once people's income reaches $60,000 a year their happiness levels do not increase as their income goes up (the study looked at US citizens). An annual income of $60,000 equates to $5,000 a month. And, as we've seen, making $5,000 a month in royalties is not that difficult once you have a modest portfolio of well-written and properly marketed books.

For a great TED talk, in which Dr Kahneman discusses happiness and income, watch this video:

ted.com/talks/daniel_kahneman_the_riddle_of_experience_v s_memory

Or use this shortened URL: **bit.ly/dktedtalk**

(The bit about the relationship between income and happiness starts at 17 minutes into the video, but it's well worth watching the whole thing.)

If you're focusing on royalties then you need to make sure that you choose a niche or genre in which you can make plenty of sales. We'll look at how to do that in the next chapter. You'll also want to consider publishing something that you can serialize for maximum royalties – we'll look at that towards the end of this chapter.

2. Expert positioning

Positioning is about how your customers, clients and prospect perceive you and/or your business.

A published book is a tremendously powerful positioning tool, especially if you can get it to bestseller status – and on Amazon it's really not that hard to do because there are so many categories, each of which has its own bestseller list!

Get your promotion right and your book should rocket to bestseller status. You may even be able to get it to the coveted #1 bestseller spot for one or more of its Amazon categories. Not only does it feel great to have a bestseller – and particularly a #1 bestseller – it instantly positions you.

Being able to say that you are a bestselling author will open a lot of doors for you. It also means that people will instantly see you as an expert on the subject of your book.

In turn, being seen an expert makes you an authority, which means that people will respect you and listen to what you have to say. That gives you a chance to build a relationship with them.

The best way to build a relationship with them is to provide value to them. Give people useful information on your topic through a website, blog, social media, email, video, webinars or podcasts. This will do two very important things: it will build trust and it will create reciprocity.

Trust is essential if you want people to buy from you. And creating reciprocity also makes it much more likely that people will buy from you. Reciprocity is hardwired into us – the more you help someone the more likely they are to help you back: in this case by buying your product, service or other books.

So, being the published author of a bestselling book gives you a platform from which to reach large numbers of people. And it opens doors. It will allow you to position yourself as a trusted authority, to build an audience and to create tremendous reciprocity with them.

Having this kind of respect and credibility is incredibly powerful for you and your business. It means that 1) people will be much more willing to buy from you, and 2) they will be prepared to pay much higher prices.

Expert positioning is important for a whole range of people – assuming they want to make the most of their career or business, as the case may be. People who can benefit from expert positioning include:

- Authors (both fiction and non-fiction)
- Teachers
- Speakers
- Coaches
- Seminar leaders
- Consultants
- Professionals
- Business owners who provide a service
- Business owners who sells a product

Whatever you do, having a book will allow you to get paid much more for your time. By positioning yourself and your business in the right way people will stop seeing what you offer as a commodity and instead see it as highly valuable.

Yes, it's great to make money on royalties, but the reality is that you can often make far more money by promoting your book to bestseller status and using the positioning that this gives you to sell your products or services on the back end. Of course, you need to have a quality product or service that relates to your book.

In fact, if you set things up right, it's actually possible to give your book away for free and still make more money than most traditional authors – as long as you have a back end product or service in place.

What I have found, however, is that readers who pay for a book are much more likely to value what you offer and convert into customers or clients than readers who get the book for free.

Even if you don't have an existing business, I would strongly recommend thinking about offering some sort of backend product or service to your readers. If you are a fiction writer you could, for example, offer to coach other writers, give creative writing classes or promote yourself as a speaker. If you are a non-fiction writer then you can still offer coaching or speaking, but you can also offer a product or service that relates to the subject covered in your book.

3. "Commission" publishing

You could become a publisher of other people's work – you, in effect, become the publishing house! This gives you tremendous leverage and allows you to rapidly build up a large portfolio of work.

There are three ways in which you can become a publisher, the first of which I call "commission" publishing and which we'll deal with here. This is when you commission a ghostwriter (or multiple ghostwriters) to write books for you.

Commissioning ghostwriters has the advantage of allowing you to have several books in production at the same time. This means that you can concentrate on the business and marketing side of publishing rather than the research and writing.

I mentioned in the "Who is this for?" section at the beginning of the book that ghost writing is a common practice in the traditional publishing industry. I also said that there is nothing wrong with hiring a ghostwriter as long as you follow the golden rule I gave you:

Your books must provide value for your readers.

Ghostwriting is, amongst other things, about leveraging the time and writing expertise of professional writers. If building a publishing business is for you then as well as working with ghostwriters you should also be looking to cut down your workload further by hiring people to proofread, edit and format the books for you once they are written. This is a powerful way of quickly building up a large portfolio of books, all of which are earning you royalties.

For more information about how to hire ghostwriters, editors and proofreaders see chapter 4 – Writing your book quickly.

4. "Content" publishing

The second way of becoming a publisher is to help other people get published on Kindle in exchange for a fee or a royalty based commission or preferably both. I call this "content" publishing because you are doing just that – finding people with content and helping them publish it.

There are lots of people with content out there who either don't know how to get it onto Kindle or wouldn't know how to promote it successfully if they did. There are others who simply don't have the time or the inclination to repurpose their content and put it into a book. Many of these people would be happy to pay you to do it for them.

If you choose to become a content publisher then your job will be to discover unpublished experts with worthwhile content. The best people for you to publish are those who already have a big following – be that on their blog, website, Facebook or Twitter, etc. It's very easy to get them ranking well when they have an existing platform and once you've got them ranking well Amazon's marketing machine will take over and keep generating sales for them – and for you.

You can either work with people directly to repurpose and repackage their content or hire an editor to work with them. Obviously, working with editors will allow you to produce books more quickly as you get to leverage other people's time.

The revenue model I recommend for content publishing is as follows:

Fee + Costs + Commission

Fee

Ideally you should charge a fee for the work that's involved, though if you are confident that the book will generate significant royalties you may want to reduce or waive the fee if that is necessary to secure the deal.

Any fee you charge will depend, ultimately, on how much you can negotiate – there is no set amount. The more you can offer your prospect in terms of your ability to position them and to successfully market their book the higher the fee you will be able to charge.

Costs

The costs of creating the book – editorial work, proofreading, formatting and cover design – should be taken from the revenue generated by the book. To make this more attractive to your prospect these costs can be incurred at your risk. In other words, you will cover the costs upfront and then recoup the amount spent from the initial book royalties.

Commission

Finally, we have the commission element of your revenue. Typically, this will be around 30% of royalties. Note that you will be getting 30% of royalties and not 30% of the book's price. Assuming that the book is priced to fall in the 70% royalty bracket your commission would be as follows:

70% x 30% = 21% (of retail price)

It is through the commission model that you truly align your interests with those of your client. A good book that is well marketed will create long-term financial rewards for both of you.

5. "Traditional" publishing

When I say "traditional" publishing I'm talking about a business model in which authors request your help to publish and promote their books, much in the way that authors (or usually their agents) approach traditional publishing houses.

While anyone can now self-publish that does not mean that all prospective authors have the inclination to. Many authors simply love to write and have no real desire to get involved in the intricacies of formatting, publishing, managing and promoting their books.

Similarly, business people who wish to have a book as a positioning tool will frequently not want to get involved in the behind-the-scenes work and the marketing activities – they are simply too busy working on (or in) their business. In fact, you may well find that you have to combine both the content and traditional publishing models as many business people will have neither the time nor the inclination to write their own book.

This provides you with a great opportunity if you wish to offer this sort of publishing service. You can easily find authors in online writers' groups and forums – there are many writers' groups on Facebook, for example. Business owners can be approached directly or through business organizations.

In terms of getting prospects to discover you the usual rules apply: build a website or blog and market yourself; build up your social media presence; speak to relevant organizations.

The revenue model for traditional publishing is the same as for content publishing: fee + costs + commission.

6. Product/affiliate sales

One of the great things about a Kindle book is that you can include links. And those links can be to products or services that you sell or products and services that you're an affiliate for.

You have to be careful here. Fill your book with too many product/affiliate links and at least some of your readers will see them as spam, get upset with you and leave bad reviews, which will definitely hurt your long-term sales.

Use product/affiliate links sparingly. And make sure to use them in a way that genuinely serves people. In other words only link to products that you have used or would use and that you can honestly recommend as helpful to them in the context of why they are reading the book.

Best practice (as well as being FTC compliant) is to be fully transparent and actually tell people if you are going to get paid as a result of them buying through a product/affiliate link. Your readers will certainly appreciate your honesty and if they like the product you're recommending there's every chance they'll go ahead and buy it anyway.

This monetization method is most suited to non-fiction books, particularly "how to" books that help solve some sort of problem.

7. List building

A more subtle way of selling to people is to use your Kindle book to build a list of email subscribers. This method is great both for fiction writers who want to sell more books (you can email your list every time you launch a new book) and for non-fiction writers selling any sort of backend product or service including, of course, more books!

You may have heard the Internet marketing saying that "The money is in the list." This is only partially true – the real truth is that "The money is in your relationship with your list." Add great value to your list, build great rapport and reciprocity and you'll have a great relationship with them. Then they'll be happy to look at and buy your products, services or recommendations.

The strategy for building your list is simple: you include (at least) one Call to Action (CTA) in your book that offers some kind of lead magnet, also known as an ethical bribe, in exchange for your reader's email. It might be a video training, a free report or a resources guide that relates to the subject matter of your book. If you are a fiction writer you might offer a free short story or background notes on your characters. Whatever you choose to offer it should be something that is genuinely interesting or valuable to your readers.

In order to get it they must respond to your CTA by clicking on the link in your book. This will take them to what is known as a squeeze page – a web page where they can opt-in to get the freebie. You collect their email using what is known as an autoresponder and build your list, while the autoresponder – as the name suggests – automatically sends them an email giving them access to their free digital gift. You build your list; they get something cool and valuable for free!

The autoresponder that I use and recommend (I have tried several) is **GetResponse.com** with prices starting at just $15 per month for 1,000 subscribers.

Autoresponder services like GetResponse work hard to ensure that their services are in compliance with CAN-SPAM and other relevant legislation, however, you also have a responsibility to only email people who have chosen to opt-in to your list. A good autoresponder service will automatically include a link with each email that allows people to opt-out if they no longer wish to receive your emails.

Setting up your squeeze page

If you intend to build a list (and I strongly recommend you do) then you will need to set up a squeeze page to which you can send people.

I'm not going to get into a lot of detail about how to build squeeze pages or how to use autoresponders as it's beyond the scope of this book. Plus there is plenty of information available online if you're not sure how to do this.

What I will do, however, is make a recommendation. I have used a variety of services to create squeeze pages or to build them on my own websites. However, the one that I use most often now is **LeadPages.net** (note that is .net not .com).

I like LeadPages because it is both quick and easy as well as being very inexpensive – at the time of writing it's just $37 a month to create as many squeeze pages as you want. In fact, if you opt for annual billing it works out at less than $25 a month.

8. Bulk sales

Bulk sales are, by definition, a great way of selling lots of books at once. A friend of mine recently sold 1,000 copies of her coaching book to a large company for them to give out to all of their executives. It's possible to shift hundreds, thousands or even tens of thousands of books this way.

Selling your book in this way is also great positioning and a tremendous endorsement. In the example I've just given the author is now known to every executive in that company, all of whom now recognize her as an expert in her field. And she made thousands of dollars in royalties "overnight" into the bargain!

I put "overnight" in quotation marks because, of course, the author in fact worked very hard to get the book written and published and also had to work hard to build a relationship with the company's executives and get the deal setup. However, you get the idea and I'm sure you can see how powerful this monetization method can be.

The books can be purchased as electronic downloads (this can be done through Amazon's Whispercast). Or, to increase the perceived value (and price point) of your book, you can use Amazon's CreateSpace to order print-on-demand physical copies.

And if you can achieve bestseller status before you set up the deal that will make it a whole lot easier.

Bulk sales do not just apply to corporate buyers. The trick is to look for organizations — be they local, national, corporate, non-profit, voluntary, religious — that are aligned in some way with the topic of your book. It is possible to set up bulk sales for both fiction and non-fiction books, you simply have to find the right audience.

Recap...

So far we have eight different ways that you can monetize Kindle books. It's really important to spend some time thinking about which one/s are right for you before you start writing or publishing. And remember that you can monetize your books in multiple ways.

9. Serialization

Strictly speaking serialization should come under marketing not monetization, but I'm going to bring it in early and cover it here because it is such a powerful way of increasing your royalties. Also, it will be helpful for you to be aware of the power of serialization as we progress through the book.

Clearly, the more books you sell the more royalties you will make and one of the best ways to sell more books is to... wait for it... write more books!

OK, now I know that sounds painfully obvious, but this goes way beyond just having more books on sale. If someone reads one of your books and enjoys it they are several times more likely to buy your other books than someone who hasn't discovered you yet. Think about your own favorite authors — how many of their books do you own? If you're like me it's most or all of them.

Serialization can mean a number of different things and can be used for both fiction and non-fiction books.

First of all, it can mean writing a series of books that follow on from or relate to each other in some way.

The Harry Potter series is a great example, in which the second book in the series picks up where the first left off and so on. Each book has its own stand-alone narrative arc, but there is also a wider, overarching narrative arc that links the books in the series. Worldwide the seven Harry Potter books have sold over 450 million copies and counting.

Another great recent example is in erotica with "Fifty Shades of Grey" – first released as an eBook in May 2011. The original book is now part of a trilogy together with "Fifty Shades Darker" and "Fifty Shades Freed". The books in the series have topped bestseller lists around the world, together selling over 100 million copies. A somewhat different target audience to Harry Potter, but still incredibly successful!

You might create a character that appears in a series of books. Each book is a standalone story and, unlike our Harry Potter example, not linked by an overarching narrative arc (though previous exploits may well be referred to). However, the main character and usually a number of supporting characters stay the same. This has been done with great success in detective novels – think Sherlock Holmes or Hercule Poirot!

Then there is the formulaic approach to serialization like that taken by romance publisher Mills and Boon. While the books are not serialized in the strict sense, buyers keep coming back for more because they know exactly what to expect and like what they are getting. Instead of continuing an existing story or writing about established characters it is the successful formula that creates repeat buyers.

In the non-fiction space, serialization might mean a training guide or "how to" advice series in which each volume covers a different stage in the training. For example, if you wanted to teach people about social media then rather than a single large book you could have separate volumes on Facebook, Twitter, Pinterest, YouTube, etc. Another example would be a niche travel guide with separate volumes for different cities or countries.

Whichever method of serialization you choose, what matters is that people who buy and enjoy the first book in the series are likely to buy and enjoy the second and the third and so on. That way a single customer can generate multiple sales meaning much higher revenues.

You may want to sell the first book in your series at a low price to build your fan base and sell subsequent books at a higher price, for example, $0.99 for your first book and then $2.99 for the rest in the series.

Make sure that at the end of your books you provide links to the other books in that series so that a) your readers know about them, and b) you make it as easy as possible for them to buy. Very often, because they want to keep on reading, people will simply click on the link to your next book and download it immediately: instant gratification – one of the great advantages of Kindle!

Serialization also means that Amazon will cross-promote your books when people buy them. We've all seen how, when you search for or buy books, Amazon will show you similar books that were "Also Bought" by other customers. How many times have you ended up buying an extra book or books because of this? It's a very effective strategy and it's exactly what Amazon will be doing for your books if you serialize them.

Final thoughts

OK, so I've just given you some important things to think about – nine ways to monetize your book, including the importance of serialization as a way of boosting your sales. These are things you want to think about before you create your first book – why are you writing it? How are you going to monetize it? Will your book fit into your existing business if you have one and if so how? Will you be monetizing your book in multiple ways?

In the next chapter we'll look at how to choose a niche or genre where there will be plenty of demand for your book.

Chapter 3:
Choosing your niche or genre

In this chapter we're going to look at how to choose your niche (if you're writing non-fiction) or genre (if you're writing fiction).

To get the biggest bang for your buck (or at least your time) you'll want to choose a niche or genre in which you can generate lots of sales. There are certain niches and genres that consistently outsell others and it's worth knowing what these are.

Of course, you may already have a topic or idea that you're just burning to write about, which is great. Just bear in mind that if it does not have mass appeal you may limit your financial success.

Fiction or non-fiction?

Amazon don't publish detailed figures for which books are selling best on Kindle, so no one knows exactly what the break down is between fiction and non-fiction.

The consensus is that fiction outsells non-fiction and the overall Kindle bestseller list seems to bear this out. Last time I checked it 93 of books on it were fiction, while only 7 were non-fiction.

Having said this, however, it really shouldn't make any difference to what you choose to write for the simple reason that sales in both markets are absolutely huge!

What's more important is picking a good niche or genre within the market you choose and writing about something that interests you. So go ahead and choose from fiction or non-fiction based on what you feel most comfortable with and what you will most enjoy working on.

Choosing your niche or genre

A great way to get good ideas for your niche or genre is to go to Amazon and look at the Kindle bestseller lists for the areas that interest you. There are, in fact, many Kindle bestseller lists and Amazon organizes them according to the following hierarchy:

1. First of all there is the overall bestseller list – the top 100 books on Kindle.

2. Next you have the bestseller lists for fiction and non-fiction. Again, as with all Amazon's bestseller lists, we are talking about the top 100 books in each case.

3. Below this you have Amazon's top level categories, which will sit underneath either fiction or non-fiction. At the time of writing there are 27 top level categories on Amazon.com, though both the number of categories and the categories themselves vary from time to time. Each top-level category has its own bestseller list.

4. Finally, underneath the top-level categories there are various sub-categories. There may be several sub-categories underneath a single top-level category, with each sub-category having its own bestseller list.

Oh, and to add an extra layer of complication, there are actually two lists in each case: top 100 paid and top 100 free. (We'll talk about why on earth you'd want to give your book away for free in chapter 9.)

As you browse through the bestseller lists what recurring themes do you see? What books are both popular and the sort you'd like to write? Or, if you are going down the commission publishing route, what sort of books might you want to outsource to a ghostwriter based on their popularity?

If you need them there will be no shortage of ideas for you to discover on the various Kindle bestseller lists. However, let's take a look at some of the perennial favorites, starting with non-fiction and then moving on to fiction:

Non-fiction

Let's start with what are known as the three non-fiction "mega-niches".

These mega-niches are:
1. Health and fitness
2. Money and business
3. Dating and relationships

What you will find is that most of the major niches in the non-fiction space are in fact sub-niches of one of the three mega-niches. As you read through the following list of non-fiction niches that are popular on Kindle you'll see what I mean:

Business

Starting a business, buying a business or franchise, running a business, marketing a business, managing a business, selling a business – there are many sub-categories of business books to cover the many aspects of setting up and running a business.

Someone who has invested huge amounts of time and money in their business is highly motivated to see it succeed and will happily pay for advice that will help them.

The same goes for people who are desperate to start a business because of a desire to get rich or to escape a job that they hate.

Making money

There are always plenty of people looking for ways to make more money and to do it faster and easier. Becoming rich and/or financially free is a very seductive idea that will never grow old. One caveat here, however: please don't go promoting "get rich quick" schemes. Remember, your books should always deliver real value.

Investing

What do you do with your money once you've made it? How do you keep it safe? How do you make it grow? How do you get enough money together for the kid's college fund and for retirement? This is a big deal for a lot of people.

Personal development

This is a huge category encompassing many things. Here are some examples: over-coming fear; increasing confidence; goal setting; achieving more; time management; ending procrastination; better communication; career development; influence; motivation; relaxation; over-coming stress.

Dating

You can't have a relationship until you've got the dating thing worked out so the need to get it right is a powerful motivator that sells a lot of books.

Examples topics might include: how to get a date in the first place; how to have a successful date; or, how to transition from dating to a relationship. They could be aimed at men or at women. They could be aimed at young people or divorcees getting back into the dating game.

Relationships

This could include anything from how to have a great relationship to how to save a failing one or how to escape a bad one. How to have a great relationship in bed is another popular niche.

Marriage

With marriage we are still really under the relationship heading and so the same things could be covered here, to which can be added dealing with and managing divorce.

Religion and spirituality

If this appeals to you there are some highly motivated buyers out there for whichever major religion or spiritual philosophy you want to write about.

Health

Part of the health and fitness mega-niche, health is a huge niche in its own right – the list of health related topics is almost endless.

Fitness

Fitness is the other half of the health and fitness mega-niche. Again, it is huge in its own right with countless different approaches to keeping fit that appeal to different ages, sexes and demographics and with new approaches being invented all the time.

Weight loss

Weight loss is a monster sub-niche of the health and fitness mega-niche. As more and more people in the world become overweight, obese and diabetic this is a niche that is going to grow and grow.

Nutrition

Some people read about nutrition because they need help with a particular allergy or illness. Others study nutrition because they are fanatical about their health. For others it might be about optimizing their sporting performance. All these types are highly motivated buyers and this is a great area for niching down into specific topics, which you can then cross-promote.

Fiction

When it comes to fiction the undisputed heavyweight champ of the genres is romance. Remember earlier when I said that, last time I checked, 93 of the top 100 books on Kindle were fiction? Well, 45 of those 93 fiction books were romance – that's an amazing 48%. So, if you're fiction writer who wants to write romance novels things are looking very good for you!

Here are some of the most successful fiction genres on Kindle:

Romance

Romance is, always has been and always will be a huge seller and you'll see loads of romance novels in the bestseller lists.

Erotica

We've already talked about how the Fifty Shades trilogy, which started as an eBook, has sold over 60 million copies. This is a genre that has exploded in popularity in the last few years as it's become much more mainstream.

Mystery and thriller

This is another huge selling genre and perennial favorite. Think of authors like John Grisham and Dan Brown.

Fantasy

Here you get to write about wizards, dragons, knights, goblins and orcs or whatever fantasy world your mind can conjure. Here are some examples of fantasy book series that have done quite well for themselves: Lord of the Rings, Harry Potter and Game of Thrones!

Young adult

This genre includes fiction designed to appeal to readers ranging in age from early teens all the way up to those in their early twenties. Note that this genre contains sub-divisions – books that will appeal to those in their early teens are unlikely to appeal to those in their early twenties.

The key to young adult literature is that the protagonist should be someone of a similar age as the target readership and who will likely to be dealing with the sort of stage of life issues that the readership is familiar with.

Horror

Paranormal, vampires, zombies, ghosts, psychos and serial killers – think Stephen King who has published over 50 novels that together have sold over 350 million copies!

Combining genres

You can also do fantastically well by combining two or more of these popular fiction genres. For example the incredibly successful Twilight series is described in Wikipedia as "vampire themed fantasy romance young-adult fiction".

So, there's an example of four genres rolled into one: romance; fantasy; horror; and young-adult. It seems to have worked with the series selling over 116 million books worldwide!

Summary

We've touched on a wide range of different niches in both the fiction and non-fiction categories. And the lists we've just gone through are not exhaustive – really they're a starting point to get you thinking about which niches or genres are right for you.

And don't get too hung up on your niche or genre, because you can always change it later if it's not working out for you or if you decide you'd prefer to be writing or publishing something else.

The important thing is that you pick one and get started.

This is where the rubber meets the road. And it's also something that a lot of people turn into a much bigger deal than it should be: they start worrying about getting things perfect first time.

If that sounds at all familiar you need to know something... things are never perfect. Please don't get too hung up on exactly what to write. Pick a niche or genre that appeals to you, spend some time researching it and then come up with an idea and get to work.

You'll learn ten times more from the time you spend getting a book written and published (whether you write it yourself or hire a ghostwriter – it doesn't matter) than you ever will thinking about it and worrying about getting it perfect.

And after you've written your first book the second one will be much easier, probably get written a lot faster and it will likely be a better book. And the third will be easier still...

Once that first book is done you're on a roll. But, that's only because you got started in the first place. Once you get going it's easy to build up a portfolio of books all making you royalties and generating income – much easier than you think. Just take that first step!

Oh, and the more you practice the better you get. Just like everything else that's worthwhile in life. And that brings us nicely to the next chapter – how do you write your book quickly?

Chapter 4:
How to write your book quickly

In this chapter we're going to look at how to get your book written quickly.

The chapter is organized as follows:

Part I: Writing best practices

Part II: The 7 Step (Non-Fiction) Research System

Part III: The 5 Step (Fiction) Research System

Part IV: The 10 step Writing System

Part V: Hiring a ghostwriter

Part VI: Content editing, copy editing and proofreading

Part I looks at how to create the conditions and habits that will help you to write quickly. Part II covers the 7 step non-fiction research system I've developed that will allow you to quickly get to grips with your subject matter. Part III does the same for fiction writing only using a different 5 step research system. Part IV is where I take you through my 10 step writing system. Part V shows you how to successfully outsource a book project to a ghostwriter. Finally, Part VI takes you through the all-important editing process.

Part I: Writing best practices

I strongly believe that the key to successful writing is block time. Block time is, as the name suggests, when you set aside a block of time to work on a particular project or activity completely uninterrupted – no distractions. That means no emails, messages or phone calls. It means no one interrupting you for a chat or to ask you a quick question. It means doing nothing during that block of time except working on your writing.

Block time and flow

Block time is how books get written quickly. It's also the key to being productive whatever you are doing. The more we are distracted the less we get done – that much is obvious. What is less obvious is that even when we go back to our primary task our minds remain partly distracted and can take several minutes to become fully focused again.

We work best when we are in a state of "flow" – a concept first described by renowned psychologist Mihály Csíkszentmihályi. Flow can be described as a state of concentration in which a person is completely absorbed in the activity at hand, such that they become unaware of what's going on around them. When you are in a state of flow time really flies! Sometimes it is also described as being "in the zone".

If you are in a state of flow and you get interrupted it can take as much as fifteen minutes to get back into a flow state, depending on the nature of the interruption. That is a lot of time to be working at reduced productivity. And every time you get interrupted your productivity drops again.

Unfortunately, being constantly interrupted is the default state for most of us. There are always multiple jobs that need doing. There's always someone emailing us, messaging us, calling us, or stopping by to chat: all wanting a piece of our time; all stealing away a little bit of our productivity – and therefore stealing from our earning power.

The solution is not that difficult. It just requires a little bit of setting up and a little bit of discipline. But once you've set things up so that you can work in block time you'll never want to go back to the way things were! (If you're already working in block time then you know what I mean.)

Creating block time

There are three keys to creating block time and none of them are that difficult. They are:
1. Choosing a time
2. Managing your environment
3. Managing people

1. Choosing a time

The first thing you need to do is decide when you're going to set up your block time. Personally, I like to set up my block time for the first couple of hours of my working day when I'm the most mentally and physically fresh and therefore the most productive.

However, I will also work in block time at other times of the day if possible, *in addition to my morning session*. The important thing is that you set up at least one consistent time when you can work – whether it is morning, afternoon or evening is a question of personal preference. Being consistent will help when it comes to step 3 – managing people.

2. Managing your environment

Managing your environment means three things. First, it means eliminating distractions; second, it means having everything you need for your work at hand; and third, it means making sure you are physically comfortable.

Eliminating distractions means turning off your email and any instant messaging services you have running. It means putting your mobile on silent in a place where you can't see it if someone rings in and diverting or muting your landline. It means shutting down Facebook and Twitter.

It can also mean eliminating distractions in the space where you work. Are there things that will distract you if they catch your eye? If so put them somewhere else.

Once you've eliminated your distractions you need to get your work space set up so that you have everything that you need ready and to hand. You don't want to be jumping up every few minutes to fetch something.

Everything you need to work efficiently and effectively should live in your work space so that it's set up and ready to go every time you're ready to start your block time. It should also be tidy so that things are easy to find – if you're someone who struggles with tidiness it is well worth making the effort to do this.

Finally, make sure your environment is comfortable so you're not being distracted by being too hot, too cold, too hungry, to thirsty, too cramped, etc.

By the way, it's not a good idea to eat lots of carbs before sitting down to try and write. After a high carb meal the brain produces serotonin, which is a hormone that helps send you to sleep.

3. Managing people

This is the hardest part of the set up, but even this isn't really that difficult. It just requires setting some ground rules and managing expectations.

You can't have block time if people are interrupting you. So you need to explain to the people around you that at certain times of day you are not to be disturbed unless there is a genuine emergency.

For example, my daily block time session runs from 9am to 11am. During that time my staff know not to call me (I run a virtual office) or to put calls through to me and they know that I won't be responding to any emails until later. They also know that if there's something really important and urgent that they can reach me, but they almost never need to – it turns out most things can wait a couple of hours!

Consistency

It's not uncommon to get more done in two hours of uninterrupted block time than in the whole of a normal day. So now you've got your block time set up you want to get consistent with it.

Ideally you want to schedule your block time for the same time each day for five or six days a week, with at least one day off to refresh and recharge yourself. If you can do this you'll find you start to get phenomenal results and your productivity will go through the roof.

And of course, the more block time you can set up the more productive you will become and the faster your books will get written.

How long does it take to write a book?

This is a question I am often asked – how long does it take to write a book? Well... how long is a piece of string?

It depends on so many factors. How long will your book be? How well do you know your subject and how much research do you need to do? How complicated is your subject matter or plot? How many hours a day will you be writing and how focused are you when you do write?

In a full day I might expect to get an average of 2,000 to 3,000 words written, but the actual amount varies greatly depending on the complexity of the subject matter and whether I need to do any additional research.

On a tough subject that I'm researching while I write I might struggle to hit 1,000 words. On the other hand, if I'm writing about something I know well and there's no extra research required I might manage 4,000 words or more.

As a very rough rule of thumb you can estimate 200 to 250 words to a page for a Kindle book or 300 to 350 words to a page for a hardcopy. But remember, Kindle screen sizes vary and people can change the font size so this is very approximate guide.

So if I have a 2,000 word day that would equate to around 8 to 10 pages of a Kindle book. And since Kindle books can be much shorter than traditional books (though they don't have to be) I can get a short book written in one to two weeks.

Bear in mind though, that this doesn't include any time spent on research before starting the writing process itself – which we'll look at in a moment. Also, don't forget, writing is a skill and the more you practice it the faster you'll get.

How long should a Kindle book be?

Another question I get asked a lot is how long should a Kindle book be?

The simple answer is this: as long as it needs to be to fulfil on the promise you made to your readers when you asked them to buy the book.

Beyond that, the rules for Kindle books are a little different from traditional books – partly due to the pricing system and partly due to the ease and speed of publishing.

As you know Amazon encourages us to price our Kindle books at between $2.99 and $9.99 to take advantage of the 70% royalty bracket. This means that Kindle books are nearly always sold at lower prices than physical books.

In a reflection of this lower pricing, self-published Kindle books are often shorter than traditionally published books. The Kindle book buying public are quite used to this and don't expect to get the same for $2.99 on Kindle as they would if paying, for example, $19.99 in a bookstore.

Having said this, it's important to stress that the Kindle book buying public are only OK with this providing that the following three conditions are met:

1. The book, regardless of length, has genuine merit – in other words, you provide value to your readers.
2. The book delivers on its promise (the "promise" is the title, sub-title, cover, description and editorial reviews taken together – in other words, the materials that influence people to buy the book in the first place).
3. The length of, and value provided by, the book is genuinely reflected in the price.

Get these things right and it doesn't matter if your book is 10,000 words long, 50,000 words long or 200,000 words long. What I would recommend, however, is that as a rule of thumb you don't publish anything that's less than 10,000 words. It's just my opinion, but selling a book that's too short is setting people up for disappointment – which is tantamount to asking for refunds, complaints and bad reviews.

Part II: The 7 Step (non-fiction) research system

There are lots of systems for both researching and writing books. The research system I'm giving you here is the one that I like to use and which I've developed over time. It works well for me and I think it will serve you, but don't be afraid to incorporate new ideas of your own or ideas from other systems (this goes for the systems in Parts III and IV as well). It's all about finding what works best for you.

The system works particularly well for "how to" non-fiction books that solve problems for people. Here's an overview of the system:

1. Read at least 5 bestselling books on your subject
2. Look at the contents pages of multiple books for common themes
3. Review the top blogs and advice websites on your topic
4. Survey customers/potential customers and browse forums
5. Interview experts
6. Set out your FAQs and SAQs
7. Use Google to fill in any blanks

Now let's go through each of these steps in turn.

1. Read at least 5 bestselling books

Read at least 5 bestselling books on your topic. The more books you read the more you'll know about your topic, but you'll also suffer from the law of diminishing returns.

I like to use the Pareto or 80/20 Principle when I'm working. That means finding the 20% of effort that will still generate 80% of the results.

Use your judgment, but the chances are that 5 good books on your topic will give you 80% of the results that you would get from reading 10 books. Spend your time wisely.

2. Look at contents pages of multiple books for common themes

The "Look Inside" feature on Amazon is great for this. You might only read 5 books on your topic, but you can quickly browse many more and see what their authors thought was important enough to include.

Looking at chapter summaries, bullet points, highlighted sections and action lists is a great way of finding common themes and important points. You may need to go into a bookstore to do this as the Look Inside feature only allows limited browsing.

3. Review the top blogs and advice websites on your topic

Like reading bestselling books, there's not an exact number of blogs and websites that you should look at. Again, use the 80/20 Principle and pick only the most important ones as the law of diminishing returns applies here too.

4. Survey customers/potential customers and browse forums

If you have a list of customers or a way of reaching potential customers then you can use **SurveyMonkey.com** for free to create and send out a survey to them. Use the survey to ask them what they'd like to know about your topic and what's important to them.

Two great questions to ask are:

1. "What's your number one question regarding [your topic]?"

2. "What's your number one problem regarding [your topic]?"

Browsing forums will also give you lots of ideas for the questions and problems that most frequently come up for people.

5. Interview experts

There are two reasons for interviewing experts. One is to gather research for your book. The other is as a way of actually getting your book written. In other words, you record the interviews and have them transcribed. Each transcribed interview then becomes a chapter of your book.

Either way, you should leave the expert interviews until after you have gone through steps 1 to 4, that way you'll ask better questions and get much more from the interviews. Also, it's a good idea to have read the expert's book if they've got one.

If you're using interviews to write your book (rather than for research) you will need to make it very clear to the experts you are interviewing that this is what you intend to do *at the time you are setting up the interviews* and get their agreement. To be on the safe side it's a good idea to save email correspondence with them to this effect.

You will need to record the interviews and get them transcribed. Once you've done that review the transcriptions and make any edits needed to clarify things or to remove irrelevant material (or hire an editor to do this – see chapter 4). Once you've done that send a copy of the edited transcript to your interviewee to get their input and approval.

Five to ten expert interviews, with each one forming a separate chapter, and perhaps with some additional commentary by you, would make an excellent book.

It's a good idea to talk to experts who will give a range of different viewpoints or cover different areas of the topic so that each chapter adds value in a different way.

6. Set out your FAQs and SAQs

I have to give full credit for this idea to Mike Koenigs who is a great teacher when it comes to both video and online marketing and an all-round outstanding guy!

The first time I saw Mike speak was in 2009 at the very first Ultimate Business Mastery Summit, run by Chet Holmes and Tony Robbins. Immediately after the event I signed up for Mike's email list and I highly recommend you do the same if you're not on it already. You can find out more about Mike and get onto his list by going to **MikeKoenigs.com**.

FAQs are, as I'm sure you know, frequently asked questions. What are the questions people ask most frequently about your topic?

SAQs are "should ask questions". These are the questions that people should be asking, but they don't know enough about your topic to know what they don't know! What are the most important SAQs on your topic?

FAQs are important to answer and people will expect you to do that. But SAQs take your content to a whole new level. By definition, these are not things that your readers will expect answers to. By highlighting their importance and by answering those questions you set yourself apart as a true expert.

7. Use Google to fill in any blanks

Don't wait until you know everything before you start writing, otherwise you never will. Use the 80/20 Principle as discussed earlier and once you've got 80% of the information you need then get writing.

If you find there are any blanks in your knowledge once you start writing then chances are that a few Google searches will be able to fill them in (see step 6 of The 10 Step Writing System, below).

Part III: The 5 Step (fiction) research system

The research requirements for writing fiction are different from non-fiction, but no less demanding. In fact, fiction books often require an incredible amount of research – particularly if they are historical or highly technical in nature.

I'm afraid that if you're writing a novel that requires lots of research I can't change that fact, but what I can do is give you a 5 step system that will help make the process easier. Here's an overview of the system:

1. Get really familiar with your genre
2. Research as needed: it's never been easier

3. Visit places if you can
4. Interview experts and people who've "been there and done that"
5. Get started and fill in the blanks later

Now let's go through each of these steps in turn (some of the points may seem obvious, but they still need to be mentioned!).

1. Get really familiar with your genre

If you're an aspiring fiction writer then it's a pretty sure bet that you spend a lot of your time reading. So, chances are you're already familiar with the genre you plan to write in. To the extent that you're not, spend some time immersing yourself in reading books similar to those you plan to write. This investment of your time will be well worth it in the long run.

2. Research as needed: it's never been easier

The Internet and Google have made research easier than ever before. Source material that previously needed to be ordered in advance (so it could be brought up from archives) and which could only be read within the confines of the academic library that held it (assuming you had access to that library in the first place) can now be found on the Internet with a simple search and a few mouse clicks. Of course, not everything can be accessed so easily, but you should be able to find a great deal of the information you need this way.

3. Visit places if you can

You can find out a lot through the Internet, but sometimes you'll want to visit places to get the necessary level of authenticity into your writing. When you do take photos, take video, make lots of notes and talk to the locals to really get the flavor of the place.

4. Interview experts and people who've "been there and done that"

Sometimes you'll need to interview experts on the technical or historical aspects of your book – you won't find everything you need on the Internet. You may also want to interview people who've "been there and done that" – people who've experienced what you're writing about first hand whether that's a particular event or a particular time in history.

When you interview people make sure you record the interviews and get them transcribed. No amount of note taking will capture everything that you might need so you want to have a record.

5. Get started and fill in the blanks later

Don't get so hung up on your research that you never get started!

Follow the 80/20 Principle and once you've got 80% of the information you need get writing. Of course you will find as you write that there will be blanks in your knowledge, but you can come back and fill them in later – this is a much more efficient way to write (see step 6 of The 10 Step Writing System, below).

Part IV: The 10 Step writing system

This system works for both fiction and non-fiction. Where there are elements that are specific to one sort of writing or the other I'll highlight them as we go through. Here's an overview of the system:

1. Brainstorm: get your ideas onto paper
2. Highlight key ideas and themes
3. "Chunk Up" your ideas
4. Mind map them
5. Get started!
6. Use square brackets
7. Review, proof and edit
8. Final edit and proof

    9.   Add front and back material

   10. Add your CTAs

Note that steps 7 (review, proof and edit) and 8 (final edit and proof) are what I would describe as the "minimum requirements" when editing your book – essentially what you would do if editing it yourself. For information on how to get your book professionally edited see Part VI.

Now let's go through each of these steps in turn.

1. Brainstorm: get your ideas onto paper

You've done your research, you've got lots of notes, now's the time to get all your different ideas out of your head and onto a piece of paper.

The trick with brainstorming is not to censor yourself. Get every idea down –even the ones you're not sure about. You can always get rid of them later.

2. Highlight key ideas and themes

Once you've got all your ideas down go through them and highlight the key ideas and themes. In the case of non-fiction, these are the sorts of things that will likely end up forming the basis for chapters or sections of the book. In the case of fiction, it will help you get clear on the different elements of your plot as well as your characters and how they relate to one another.

3. "Chunk Up" your ideas

This is an idea that comes from NLP (neuro-linguistic programming) and which I first learned from Tony Robbins.

Having completed steps 1 and 2 you have a piece of paper with lots of ideas on it of which you have highlighted the most important. If you go through them you'll find that certain ideas relate to one another. Group together those ideas that are related.

This will do two things: First, it will make things less overwhelming – you might go, say, from 100 separate ideas down to 10 idea groups. Second, once you have your idea groups it will really help you to work out the structure of your book, the chapters you will include and how everything fits together.

4. Mind map them

Now that you've chunked your ideas it's time to mind map them.

I love mind mapping and there is plenty of free or inexpensive software available that will allow you to do it. Or you can go old school and use a pen and paper, but trust me – software is easier and way quicker once you get used to it!

Mind mapping gives you tremendous flexibility to map out your different book sections, chapters and sub-sections within chapters. And you can keep moving things around until you're completely happy with them.

It also gives you something that's visual and color coded, which can be a big help in organizing your ideas and structure.

5. Get started!

Now it's time to pull the trigger and get writing! Don't get too hung up on any one section or passage. Get something down and move on. Then come back later with fresh eyes and rewrite it if you need to – you'll probably find that the wording you were looking for jumps out at you a lot more quickly second time around.

If you want to speed things up you may want to dictate your book. If so you have two options. One is to dictate it and send the audio file to a transcription service such as **Rev.com**. The other is to use transcription software.

My strong recommendation is that you use transcription software. Not only will it save you a great deal of money in the long run, but it will be a lot quicker than having to wait for someone to type up recordings for you.

If you are on a PC I recommend you use Dragon Naturally Speaking from Nuance. They offer two versions – Home and Premium. As the name suggests, Premium is more expensive, but in my opinion it's worth it. The key extra feature is that you can make recordings from anywhere using a smartphone and then, when you are back at your computer, load them up for transcription. If you're on a Mac the Mac version is called Dragon Dictate for Mac.

When you first start dictating it can take a bit of getting used to. But if you stick with it you will find it quickly becomes easier, faster and much more natural. Once you master it you can save yourself an enormous amount of time – it's way faster than typing even if you're a good typist!

Have someone interview you

An alternative to typing or dictating your book is to have someone interview you.

The interview questions will be based on the book framework that you created in steps 1 to 4. If you are someone who struggles to write or if you find the dictation process difficult there are tremendous advantages to this interview based approach – the most important of which is speed of implementation:

When someone is asking you questions about an area of your expertise it's easy to simply sit and answer those questions in a way that is relaxed and natural – as opposed to forcing yourself to write if writing is not something you enjoy. By answering questions in this way you can get your book written much faster. Not only are you able to speak much faster than you could ever type, but rather than agonizing over everything you write you simply talk about what you know.

Your answers to the interview questions are, of course, recorded. This recording is then transcribed and either you or an editor can then go through the transcription to edit and polish it to the point where it is suitable for publication. Many very successful books have been written using this method.

Even if you enjoy writing and are quite happy to dictate you may still decide that this is the best way to create your books – simply because it is such a quick way of getting a book written. You will also find that the better you know your subject matter the easier and more suitable this method of writing will be for you.

6. Use square brackets

Use square brackets to speed up your writing. Instead of getting stuck on a particular passage or a particular fact that needs researching, put that section in square brackets and move on. This helps you maintain a state of flow when you're writing and greatly speeds things up.

Later on you can come back and search for all the square brackets and do your tidying up/additional research as part of a separate writing session.

You may also want to outsource your outstanding research points so that you can have the answers ready and waiting for you. We'll look at the outsourcing process in Part V.

7. Review, proof and edit

Once you've finished writing your book the next step is to review, proof and edit what you've written.

The first person to review your work should be you. You may have been doing this as you've gone along, but you still need to review the finished work as a coherent whole. I would recommend that once you've written the first draft you leave it overnight before reviewing it as you'll do a much better job when you're fresh and rested.

Once you've reviewed it you'll want other people to look at it too. No matter how careful you are in your own review they will pick up all sorts of mistakes that you've missed.

Friends and family are great for this, however, try to choose people who will give you reasonably honest feedback. I say "reasonably" honest because it's rare indeed for a friend or family member to be completely honest – that's why getting professional editorial help is also recommended (see Part VI).

It's also a good idea to get any experts you involved in the research phase to review the relevant sections of your work for accuracy. This, of course, applies equally to fiction and non-fiction.

Another group you may want to involve at this stage are reviewers who fit the profile of your book's target market. They will be able to give you feedback on whether you've really delivered or not and may be able to suggest significant improvements before you actually publish.

During the review stage you need to politely let people know what your deadline is. They are doing you a favor, but the review process should not be something that holds the book up for long.

8. Final edit and proof

Once you've got all your reviewers' comments back you'll be able to do your final edit. After your final edit it's essential that you do a final proof, since new or edited material must never go out un-proofed!

9. Add front and back material

Now that you've got your book in final form you can create the any additional pages you need – known as front and back material –

such as a copyright notice; your contents page; preface or introduction; a postscript if appropriate; a resources section if appropriate; any acknowledgements; and so on. For more on organizing the front and back material of your book see Part IV of chapter 5.

10. Add your CTAs

You're now almost finished, but there's one last crucial step and that's to add your Calls to Action (CTAs).

Your CTAs are vital to your success. It's great that someone is reading your book, but what else would you like them to do? Would you like to send them to a website where you can capture their email in exchange for your lead magnet? Would you like to send them to the Amazon page of the next book in your series where they can make a "1-Click" impulse purchase? Would you like them to leave an Amazon review? My guess is you'd like them to do all of the above.

The great thing about Kindle books is that you can include links – someone can read your CTA, click the link associated with it and be on the page that you wanted them to see in a second; that's a very powerful thing to be able to do.

The 3 key CTAs

In my opinion there are three CTAs you should always include in your books:
1. List building CTA
2. Buy my next book CTA
3. Review request CTA

1. List building CTA

This is the most important CTA of all – both for fiction writers and non-fiction writers. This is the CTA that builds your email list and allows you to keep in touch with your fans, provide value to them and build a relationship with them.

The best place for your list building CTA is near the front of your book where the highest number of people will see it (though it can appear elsewhere in your book as well). That's because in reality a lot of people will download your book, but either not get around to reading it or not finish it.

Your list building CTA should be on its own page – in other words, there should be no other competing CTAs. There is a saying in marketing that "the confused mind says no". Give people two CTAs (at the same time) and they probably won't do either of them. Give people multiple CTAs all together and you can pretty much guarantee no response at all.

The list building CTA for this book is on the "**BONUS: Free Crush It with Kindle video series**" page. If you haven't registered for that yet I strongly recommend you do as the videos have some very useful content. To get instant access to the videos go to **bit.ly/ciwkvideos**

And, as I've just demonstrated, your list building CTA can appear elsewhere in your book where appropriate as well! :-)

2. Buy my next book CTA

As soon as you have two or more books you can start cross-promoting them. The perfect place to do this is at the end of your book – the fact that readers can buy your next book with a single click and download it instantly is perfect!

We're aiming for impulse purchases from avid readers. Very often people want to keep reading and are happy to plough straight on into your next book – this is certainly something that I've done when I've enjoyed an author's work and so have many thousands of other Kindle owners.

If your book is part of a series then the first book you should offer people is obviously the next book in that series. If your books aren't part of a series start with your most closely related books and then offer any others you have. If you have more than one series then make a particular point of promoting the first books in each of those series.

Just to be clear I recommend, if you have them, that you offer a range of book choices to your readers as you never know which will appeal. What I'm giving you here is the order in which I recommend you present those choices.

How to offer your books

More often than not you will see authors promoting their other books with nothing more than boring hyperlinks that barely get noticed unless the reader has already made up their mind that they want another book.

To make your books stand out I recommend that you add thumbnail images for each of them and that you hyperlink those images to their respective Amazon pages (adding images and hyperlinks is covered in Part II of chapter 5).

Underneath those images you should still include a text based hyperlink as well so that people can click that if they don't realize the image is linked. I recommend using bitly.com (which is free) to create shorted URLs. This makes it easier for any readers who need to type them and also allows you to track the number of clicks your cross-promotions are generating.

Another effective strategy is to include a short excerpt from one (or more) of your books. This may be from the beginning or it may be an excerpt from elsewhere in the book that is particularly interesting or exciting. Either way, the idea is to get your reader hooked in and wanting to know more and then leave them with a cliffhanger... and, of course, a link to the book!

The bottom line is that if someone likes your books they are many more times likely to buy your other books than someone who's yet to discover you. Make sure you give them the chance to make a purchase – it's one of the very best strategies there is for increasing your book sales.

3. Review request CTA

The more good reviews your book gets the more sales it is likely to make so you will want to include a review request CTA. The most logical place for this is at the end of the book – I recommend putting it on a separate page that comes after your "buy my next book" CTAs.

That said, if you need to boost your review numbers you may want to swap this order around – at least temporarily until you've got enough reviews in place.

Another reason for putting the review request CTA at the end of the book is that the people who enjoy your book enough to get to the end are a) more likely to leave a review, and b) more likely to leave a positive review than those who didn't bother to finish it.

For more on requesting reviews see steps 8 and 9 of the "building a bestseller" system in chapter 7.

Part V: Hiring a ghostwriter

While I personally prefer to write my own books there are, as discussed earlier, a number of reasons why you may want to hire a ghostwriter. The most likely reasons are as follows:

1. You feel that you need the help of a professional writer
2. You don't have the time to write your book or books yourself
3. You are building a Kindle publishing business and want to quickly develop a portfolio of books

Whatever your reason, there are certain things you need to know if the process is to go smoothly. Chief amongst these are where to find a ghostwriter and which one to hire, the contract terms on which you should hire them and how much you should pay them.

While on the face of it hiring a ghostwriter appears seductively easy, these are the things that make it harder than it looks. Plenty of people offer their writing services, but that doesn't mean they are necessarily any good and it may take you some time to find the right person. And, even when you've found them you don't want to pay over the odds for their work, which is why getting their contract terms and fees right is so important.

Let's look at each of these issues in turn, starting with where to find ghostwriters and deciding who to hire.

Finding a ghostwriter

There are many places where you can find ghostwriters and a quick Google search will turn up lots of options. However, the chances are that you will be able to find your writer from one of these places:

- oDesk.com
- Elance.com
- Craigslist
- Colleges and universities (students)
- writeraccess.com
- associationofghostwriters.org

If you're not familiar with them, oDesk and Elance are freelance websites where you can post jobs and hire freelance workers with a huge variety of different skills – amongst them writing and creative writing.

If you decide to use Craigslist then go to "Services" and then you'll see an odd looking subcategory under "Services" – write/ed/tr8 – which stands for "Write, Edit and Translate."

Through colleges and universities you will be able to find English or Journalism students, some of whom will do great work for low prices because they enjoy it and they want the experience. You can find students at local colleges, but thanks to the Internet you can also hire students from any university in the world that allows online job postings.

The Writersaccess website is a more expensive resource where you can find different specialists and negotiate projects with them.

Another place you can go to is the Association of Ghost Writers, which is a directory site for ghostwriters where you can commission individual ghostwriters. Again, this is a more expensive option than oDesk, Elance, Craigslist and college or university students.

Deciding who to hire

There's no shortage of ghostwriters who are willing to work for you. The hard part is deciding who to hire. This can be quite a time-consuming process, but once you've found a good ghostwriter – and assuming you plan on creating more than one book – it's important to treat them well so that you can hang on to them!

Unless you are lucky enough to have someone who comes highly recommended via a trusted source, here are some things you can do to maximize your chances of making a good hire.

First of all, freelance sites like oDesk or Elance will allow you to filter people on the basis of their average rating so be sure to only consider candidates with the highest ratings. You will also want to limit your search to people who are native English speakers (or whichever language your book will be written in).

You can often review a writer's portfolio on freelance websites and, if not, then ask candidates to send you samples. These, together with any filters you can put on your job search, will allow you to put together a shortlist.

Once you've made your shortlist commission a short chapter or section of around 1,000 words from each of your three leading candidates. It's very important to give each of them an identical brief and have them working on the same chapter or section so that you can do a proper comparison.

The other thing you must do when you commission this sample work is let them know it's at a fixed cost and explain why you're doing it so that they are incentivized to try and win the full project.

Finally, you want to give them the deadline. Obviously, the deadline needs to be reasonably tight – you want people who can turn things around quickly. If they don't make the deadline they are automatically disqualified.

Getting sample work from three writers will obviously increase your initial costs. However, it will save you money in the long run if it means you hire the right person first time around. And once you've got someone you trust and have a working relationship with you may be able to use them for multiple titles.

Contract terms

It's vitally important that you make the scope of your writing project as clear as possible as well are saying upfront how much you're willing to pay for it. We'll cover costs in the next section, but for now just be aware that they need to be fixed so that they don't spiral way beyond your budget.

For example, if you want a 20,000 word book that follows a particular structure then be explicit about it. In this case I might say that "I want a book that is going to be around 20,000 words. I want seven chapters covering [list the topic areas to be covered] plus an introduction and a conclusion to the book. Each chapter should be around 2,000 to 2,500 words."

Of course, the extent to which you can be specific about the content of the book will depend on how well you know your subject. The more research you've done the better you will be at commissioning projects and the more control you will have over them.

You also need to be very clear that the content must be yours once it's done: copyright belongs to you. You are contracting them to write the book for you so it's the same as an employer/employee relationship; once they do the work, it's yours because you paid for it. You need to be very clear about that.

If you're using a freelance website then this is likely to be covered in their terms and conditions, however, make sure you check them rather than assuming this is the case. Otherwise, at the very least, you need email correspondence, a contract or evidence in writing that the content is yours.

I also want to be very clear that it must be original content. This should go without saying, but you might be unlucky and get somebody who starts copying and pasting stuff from different sources or websites. It's against Amazon's terms and conditions to publish content that is not original (with the exception, subject to strict rules, of public domain works). Amazon will check for this and trying to publish unoriginal content is a great way of getting yourself banned and having your account closed down.

So, the content must be original and you need to make that clear in advance. A great way of checking that the work you receive is original is by using **Copyscape.com**. It's very cheap – currently just $0.05 per search – and it allows you to check that content is original before paying for it and publishing it.

Costs

Costs for ghostwriters vary enormously and can be anything from a hundred dollars or less to tens of thousands of dollars. As you might imagine, you get what you pay for!

That said, if you plan to monetize your Kindle books through royalties it's important not to overspend on the creation process. Fortunately, there are plenty of keen new writers who will often work for lower rates to get themselves established.

You may also be lucky enough to find an established ghostwriter who does great work and simply under-prices themselves. This is becoming more and more common as people compete online and services become commoditized.

Remember, the more you pay the harder it will be to make a profit on your book so don't get carried away on your spend. Take the time to find someone who will write you a decent book at a competitive rate – they do exist.

Conversely, if you are publishing a book as positioning tool or to promote a backend product or service then you will have more scope in terms of cost. That's because as a general rule these are much more effective ways of monetizing a book than simply relying on royalties.

So, how much should you spend?

As stressed above, your contract should specify a fixed price based on an agreed scope of work – *otherwise you have no idea what you could end up paying.*

In order to be able to fix your price you must first decide on the scope of the work you want done. As well as detailing what the book should cover/contain the scope of work must also specify the length of the book – for example: 20,000 words, plus or minus 10%.

Alternatively, you might set a minimum word length and allow the writer to go beyond this if they choose.

Having decided on the length of the book you can now price it on a cost per word basis (rather than an hourly rate) – this is how you fix your costs. This is typically done on a cost per 100 or a cost per 1,000 words.

Writers are used to contracting at fixed rates, so you're not going to upset anybody by doing this. If they're not prepared to work on this basis then they aren't the writer for you anyway, so move on; there are plenty of writers who will.

As a rule of thumb I would be reluctant to spend much *less* than $2 per 100 words, which, by way of example, would give you a cost of $400 for a 20,000 word book. Of course, the key consideration should be the quality of a writer's portfolio and sample work – don't be put off if you find a good writer who has simply underpriced themselves.

Part VI: Content editing, copy editing and proofreading

Polishing your book so that it's ready for publication is a three stage process consisting of content editing, copy editing and proofreading in that order.

It's worth noting that there is an overlap between content and copy editing and an overlap between copy editing and proofreading. If you go to five different websites for definitions of content editing, copy editing and proofreading you will find five different definitions.

For this reason, whenever you contract someone for any of these things you need to be clear on what it is you want and make sure they are clear on what's expected of them. This is especially important given that you will normally use different people for each of the three stages. You must know in advance that a) everything is going to be covered, and b) that you will not be paying for any duplication of services.

It is possible, as explained above in steps 7 and 8 of Part IV, to do your own editing and proofreading. However, I recommend that you go to the extra effort of getting professional editorial help as the extra quality it brings to your books is likely to be worth it in the long run.

Content editing

Content editing is also known as substantive editing for the reason that it deals with substantive changes to the content of your book.

Here are some examples – be aware that this is not an exhaustive list, but rather some illustrations of things content editors are likely to cover: plots and subplots; style; readability; characters; dialogue; believability of plot; the level of interest, excitement and tension that your book sustains – something that can apply to both fiction and nonfiction; whether the book is appropriate for the audience you're writing for and pitched at the right level.

These are big, substantive elements that are very important to your book's overall success.

Copy editing

Copy editing, on the other hand, is not concerned with the substantive elements, instead dealing with things like language and formatting.

You're not going to get significant revisions from a copy editor, but what you will get is somebody who goes through the grammar, spelling, punctuation and overall structure of your book. They'll check it for consistency and may check certain facts (though some content editors will look at some of the facts too – hence the importance of checking what each editor plans to cover).

Copy editors may also check your book for legality though again you will need to clarify this in advance. Just to be clear, your copy editor will not give you legal advice – that is a matter for your lawyer – but they may flag up potential legal problems that you can then seek advice on.

Proofreading

There is a significant overlap between copy editing and proofreading. This is a way I think of proofreading to get a distinction between the two: proofreading is "copy edit lite". A proofreader is not going to cover everything a copy editor will, however, they will give your book that final read through and final check before publishing.

Editing and proofreading costs

Like ghostwriting, the costs of editing and proofreading vary wildly. You could easily spend $2,000 or more for 10,000 words of extensive, high level, professional content editing. My guess is it's unlikely you want to spend that much!

My recommendation is that you use freelance sites like oDesk, Elance or Craigslist to find your editors and proofreaders. I have set out below some suggested budget ranges for the different types of work. The amounts are on a cost per 10,000 words basis.

Proofreading will cost you around $30, so it's certainly something that's worth outsourcing because it's very inexpensive and getting rid of (most of) those typos will really improve the book.

(I say "most of" because a few always seem to slip through. There are very few books I've read – including those from major publishers – where I haven't found at least one typo. If you find a typo in this one please let me know by emailing support at crushitwithkindle.com and I'll get it fixed!)

Basic copy editing to cover things like spelling, grammar and punctuation is going to be around the $100-$150 mark. If you want basic copy editing *plus* some minor rewriting and minor restructuring it's going to cost a little bit more, typically $150-$250.

If you want content editing that involves significant and substantive changes you should look to pay between $250 and $400. That might sound like a lot, but if you've got a book with the potential to bring you a recurring income of several hundred dollars or more per month it may well be worth spending a few hundred dollars to get it edited to a high standard.

Again, while you could spend $2,000 per 10,000 words I recommend applying the 80/20 Principle: if you spend $250 on the right content editor through oDesk, Elance or Craigslist you're likely to get 80% or more of what you get for $2,000 since there are some very skilled people on those sites. They're good at what they do and love what they do – they just don't charge as much for it. This allows you to get editorial work done for a fraction of what you would pay if you went to some of the big agencies.

You should be able to get some really good results at these prices. At a minimum I recommend that you spend the money for a proofreader. A copy editor will likely pay for themselves in the long run as well – readers are upset by books with basic language mistakes and this can lead to poor reviews, which will affect your sales, and refunds.

Only you can decide whether you want to spend the extra money on a content editor. If you are using the book as a positioning tool then content editing becomes more important. Also, if you are hoping to build your Kindle book sales to the point where you can secure a mainstream publisher it is more important. Conversely, a short "how-to" book for example may not require the extravagance of a content editor.

Chapter 5:
Formatting your book

In this chapter we're going to deal with what seems to be one of the biggest stumbling blocks for Kindle authors. It's an area that causes lots of confusion: how to format your Kindle books.

The chapter is organized up as follows:

Part I: Avoiding the Kindle formatting minefield

Part II: Formatting step by step using Word

Part III: Outsourcing your formatting

Part IV: Organizing your book

There are many different file formats you can use for Kindle – and that's precisely why formatting causes so much confusion. Part I shows you how you can avoid what I call "the Kindle formatting minefield" altogether.

Part II goes step-by-step through the process of formatting your book using Word, which is available for both Mac and PC. It's what I use to format nearly all of my books as well as those of my clients.

If you still don't want to format your book yourself, of if you have complicated formatting requirements then Part III shows you how you can outsource your formatting very inexpensively.

Finally, Part IV looks at how to organize your book: what materials to have at the front of your book, what materials to have at the back and what order they should be in so that you have a professional looking book when you put it on to Kindle.

Part I: Avoiding the Kindle formatting minefield

Here's a screenshot from Amazon's KDP (Kindle Direct Publishing) website, which is where you go to publish your books:

Types of Formats

Kindle Direct Publishing (KDP) lets
through the tips below for your pref

We accept the following formats:

- Word (DOC or DOCX)
- HTML (ZIP, HTM, or HTML)
- MOBI (MOBI)
- ePub (EPUB)
- Rich Text Format (RTF)
- Plain Text (TXT)
- Adobe PDF (PDF)

There are ten different file formats shown here and this is by no means an exhaustive list. Other formats you will find mentioned on the KDP site include XHTML, XML (OPF/IDPF format) and, if you are creating a comic or graphic novel, PDF (again), JPG, TIFF, PNG and PPM.

And all of this is before you consider whether you need to the additional flexibility that comes from using KF8 (Kindle Format 8) – something I'll be covering later in this chapter.

Here are two links to Amazon help pages on formatting. The first link deals with the formats listed above, while the second explains KF8. Before you follow up these links, however, I recommend you read the rest of this section as you may decide that you don't need to worry about most of these options.

kdp.amazon.com/help?topicId=A2GF0UFHIYG9VQ#mobi

Or use this shortened URL: **bit.ly/kdpformat**

amazon.com/gp/feature.html?docId=1000729511

Or use this shortened URL: **bit.ly/kf8format**

Having so many formats is confusing – how do you know which one is best for you? Personally, I've tried several different formats and had a variety of different issues. I've also used different software packages that are supposed to make things easy by doing the formatting for you and have yet to find one that is free of glitches. And if you get your formatting wrong there are a number of problems that can arise.

The first of these is that poor formatting will lead to you losing sales. If someone checks out your book using the "Look Inside" feature and it's badly formatted they may well decide not buy just because of that.

Even if they don't realize there are formatting issues before they buy, they will as soon as they open it up on their Kindle or iPad and start reading. In a scenario like this there is a much greater chance they will ask for a refund, so you're going to lose sales one way or the other.

The next thing is bad reviews: I've seen lots of books get bad reviews because of poor formatting. And even when people like the content of the book it's common to see criticism of formatting issues and a reduction in the star rating given.

Finally, here's something that you really want to avoid: people complaining to Amazon about your book. This does happen. If Amazon gets a complaint about your book's formatting they will check it out and, if they agree with the complaint, they will email you to tell you what the problem is and ask you to fix it. If you don't fix it – or if the problems are particularly bad – Amazon may remove your book from the Kindle store altogether.

Obviously, it's much better to get the formatting right in the first place. Of the various formats on offer Amazon recommends either Word or HTML. I have found that Word is the quickest and easiest solution and it's what I now use for all of my books. One advantage of Word is that it's available for both PC and Mac.

Another advantage for us as writers is that KDP is quite limited in the amount of formatting it will accept in a Word document. This works in our favor as although Word has lots and lots of features, most of them you just can't use – this makes formatting your book really quite straightforward!

Part II: Formatting step by step using Word

We're now going to go step-by-step through the process of formatting your book using Word. As I've just explained, although Word has many formatting options KDP only accepts a limited number of them. So if there is something that you can do in Word, but I don't mention it here that's because it won't convert across from Word to Kindle.

"Styles" setting and fonts

The first thing to mention is that when you open up your Word document you need to set the "Styles" Setting to "Normal" and use that for the main body of your text.

On the KDP website it says "… font sizes… set in Word do not apply." In other words, Amazon wants to manage the font size within Kindle books. They also want to make their fonts adjustable once people have downloaded the books so readers can change the font size on their personal devices.

Having said that, I would still recommend using something like 12 point Georgia for writing your manuscript, the reason being that you may want to distribute your manuscript outside of Kindle. For example, you may want to create a PDF and have it available on your website or you blog, or, you might want to have a PDF copy to send to people as a review copy or as a gift and so on.

For this 12 point Georgia hits the sweet spot: not too big on the page, but not so small it's hard to read, plus Georgia is a nice easy-to-read font.

If you decide to create a physical version of your book using Amazon's CreateSpace platform then the recommended font for that (as used in the templates CreateSpace provides and the CreateSpace version of this book) is 11 point Garamond.

Headings

Word has built-in headings. Using these headings will allow you, once you've finished your manuscript, to create a clickable table of contents (TOC). As long as you've got the right headings in place this is incredibly easy to do and it really enhances the experience of the reader because it allows them to navigate your book much more easily. In fact, if you don't have a clickable TOC in your book people are likely to complain about its absence.

I recommend, if you can, using up to three heading levels when setting up your book – in other words, you go what we call "three layers deep". You could use more levels, but it starts to get confusing for the reader if you use too many.

Use Heading 1 for chapters and main sections of the book (if the book is divided up into a number of distinct parts). Heading 2 is what you would use for main sections *within* chapters and then, finally, Heading 3 is for sub-headings below that.

Having said all this, you don't have to go three layers deep. If it makes sense to have chapter headings only then just use Heading 1 and don't worry about headings and subheadings.

"Paragraph" settings: fiction

I recommend different paragraph settings for fiction and non-fiction books.

As you can see in this non-fiction book I leave a gap between each paragraph, however, when writing fiction it is not normal to leave a gap. Here are the paragraph settings I recommend for fiction:

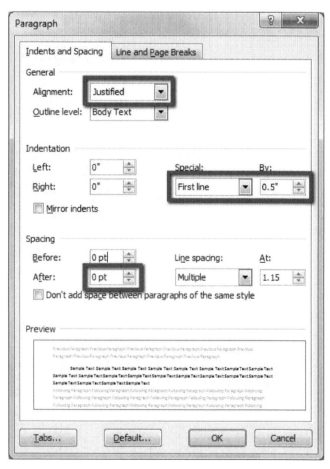

As you can see (in the bottom highlighted box) I've set the spacing in the "After" the paragraph box to zero rather than using the default setting; this eliminates the gap between paragraphs. Meanwhile, the "Before" spacing stays at zero, while the line spacing is set at "Multiple" and "1.15".

(Note this is how the settings appear in Word 2007 – on other versions of Word the appearance may vary, though the required settings will stay the same.)

I also recommend adding an indent to the first line of each paragraph. Again, you can see in the middle highlighted box that I've set a "First line" indent, which I've left at the default (½ an inch or 1.27 cm).

It's a good idea to set up that first line indent because make things easier for you as you're writing: without that indent all of your paragraphs are going to run together. When you actually upload your book to KDP Amazon will automatically indent the first line of each paragraph anyway, so it's not a requirement for Kindle – it just makes life easier for you. :-)

What about justification – should you left justify or full justify? Printed fiction books tend now to be fully justified as this cuts down on the number of pages and therefore the production costs of the book. Style manuals, on the other hand, tend to recommend left justification (also known colloquially as "ragged right") as this avoids uneven word spacing. There are some surprisingly strong opinions on this!

By default Kindle books are displayed fully justified with readers able to adjust the alignment dynamically if they choose. For the optimum reader experience this is the ideal situation.

It is still possible to change the alignment of your text if appropriate (for example, centering elements such as the title page – see below).

However, Amazon recommends that the text in the main body of your book is submitted fully justified.

If you submit text that is left or right justified Amazon will treat this as "forced alignment". This means that readers will have no choice as to how they view it, which is bound to make some of them unhappy.

As a general rule then, your text should be submitted fully justified unless you require center, left or right justification for a particular element. The top highlighted box in the screenshot shows the alignment set to "Justified".

"Paragraph" settings: non-fiction

When I write non-fiction, particularly how-to books, I like to leave a space between paragraphs. I think that breaking up the text makes the book more readable and easier to follow. Here are the settings I use for non-fiction:

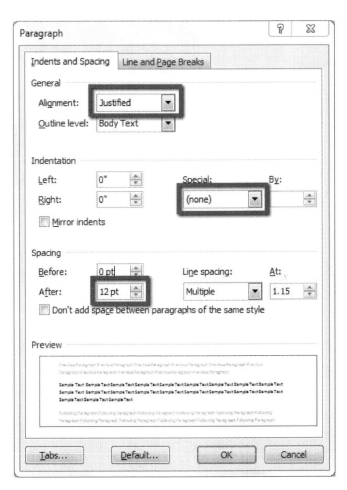

You will see that I have changed the "After" the paragraph spacing setting to 12 pt., but I have left the other spacing settings the same as the earlier fiction example.

I have also removed the first line indent by setting the middle highlighted box to "(none)" simply because indents are unnecessary when there is a space between paragraphs.

As explained above the alignment for your main body of text should be set to "Justified".

Center justification

There are a few places where it is customary to center justify a book's text.

The first of these is the title page at the beginning of your book, which should include the name of the book and the name of the author. Copyright notices are often centered as well though this is by no means a requirement. If your book has a dedication that would normally be centered as would any opening quotes. Have a look at the front of this book to see what I mean.

Indenting text

If you need to indent text it's very important not to use tabs because they won't work – they are a formatting element that doesn't translate from Word across to Kindle.

If you need to indent a section of text, you need to click on the "Page Layout" tab on the toolbar and then go across to where it says "Indent" and you can set up your left and right indents there.

Amazon prefers indenting to be used sparingly: they like the indent settings to be left as normal so that they interfere as little as possible with the way the book appears on Kindle. That said, there are times when you will want to indent text – perhaps when adding a long quote or to emphasize a particular passage. So don't be afraid to set up indents, just don't overdo it.

Spaces between sentences

I recommend using only one space between sentences rather than using double spacing as is sometimes done. Having two spaces can lead to odd looking formatting once the file is uploaded to Kindle.

If you've got double spaces in your manuscript, they're very easy to find and get rid of. All you do is open up the "Find and Replace" function in Word and in the "Find what" box you type in two spaces. Then, in the "Replace with" box you type in one space and apply this to the whole document – job done!

Bullet points

Bullet points are great for making key things stand out. Unfortunately, they are not currently supported on most Kindle formats.

However, the KF8 format, introduced in late 2012, does support bullets, though they will still only show on Kindle Fire tablets. The use of KF8 requires coding skills that are beyond the scope of this book (and indeed beyond my scope!) so if you must have bullets then I recommend you outsource your formatting – something we'll look at in Part III of this chapter.

As an alternative to bullets you can use numbered lists. You will need to switch off the automatic list formatting (a feature of Word), because automatically formatted lists will not translate across to Kindle. Instead simply type in the numbers.

Alternatively, just have lists that start with a dash. It's not quite as good as a bullet, but it will do the job.

Page breaks

At the end of a section or a chapter, don't hit "Enter" to create space as this can cause serious formatting issues on Kindle. That's because Kindle does not work with set page sizes. It can't since it has to work with many different screen sizes added to which people can vary the text size. Therefore, hitting "Enter" multiple times can lead to odd looking white space at the top of the following page.

Instead, simply insert a page break at the end of each chapter and any sections you want to follow with a new page. To do this place your cursor where you want the page break to appear, click the "Insert" tab on the toolbar in Word and then click "Page Break". That stops any white space spillovers.

Avoid importing formatting errors

It's really important not to import formatting errors. This is surprisingly easy to do if you ever copy and paste text into your document from another source.

If there's any formatting in the text you're pasting into your document that is not supported by Kindle, then it's going to cause errors when you upload your finished document to Kindle. So you want to strip out any formatting before pasting it into your document.

This is very simple to do. If you're on a PC just open up Notepad and that will automatically create a ".txt" text document for you. Then copy and paste the relevant text into your Notepad document, which will automatically strip out all the formatting. Next you copy and paste the text a second time only this time you are copying from Notepad into your Word document. Once you've done this the text will be free from any previous formatting and you can then apply your Word document formatting to it.

On a Mac it's slightly different. You open TextEdit, go to "Preferences" and under "New Document Format" click "Plain Text". Then, under the "Rich text processing" heading, turn on "Ignore rich text commands in HTML files".

Once you've done that, save those settings and then paste in the text you want to copy. The formatting will automatically be stripped out and then you can copy and paste it a second time into your Word document.

The Pilcrow

A useful feature in Word is the "Pilcrow" button — that's the one marked ¶.

It's essential, before uploading it to Kindle, that you check your manuscript for formatting errors that may have crept in like extra spaces or page breaks in the wrong place (all easily done). Clicking the Pilcrow button allows you to see all the formatting in the document and makes it much easier to pick out any errors. Once you've finished click the Pilcrow button again and the formatting notation disappears.

Images and book types

Adding images to your manuscript is very easy, but it has to be done the right way otherwise they will not display properly on Kindle.

Before I explain how to add images, however, I want to talk to you about three different kinds of books you can create on Kindle. Whether or not the method I'm about to show you will work will depend on what sort of book you want to create.

The first type of book I want to mention is a **reflowable book**. This is a term that Amazon uses to refer to what we would think of as standard Kindle books; over 95% of all books on Kindle right now are probably reflowable. This is an adjustable, flexible format that allows people to change the font size and so on. If your book is a reflowable book this method of adding images will work.

Another kind of book you can have on Kindle is a **fixed layout book**. So, for example, you might have a children's book where you've got a lot of pictures and you've got text linked to those pictures that you want to always display in a set way. For this you would want to create a fixed layout book. Creating a fixed layout book is beyond the scope of this book and, even if it were not, I would recommend you outsource the process and spend the time you save working on your next book!

Finally, in the case of **graphic novels or comics**, which are obviously very image intensive, this method will not work. So again, I recommend you outsource the process.

Adding images

It's very important never to copy and paste images into your manuscript – this will create formatting errors once you upload it to Kindle and the images will not display properly.

Instead, always insert your images. This is very easy to do: simply click the "Insert" tab on your toolbar and then click the "Picture" button. You can then select the image you want and add it to your document. Once you've done this Amazon recommends you center the image.

Image format

In most cases Amazon recommends you use JPEGs. However, for line art such as text, graphics, charts and tables, Amazon recommends GIFs. The reason for this is that JPEGs blur the sharp edges of lines or text creating fuzzy looking images.

If you have images that you need to convert to a different format you can do it for free at this website:

coolutils.com/online/image-converter

Or use this shortened URL: **bit.ly/imagecon**

Compressing images

Something else you'll want to do is compress your images. This is because if your book is in the 70% royalty bracket Amazon currently charges a download fee of $0.15 per megabyte.

This means that every time a customer downloads a copy of your book, you are getting charged based on the file size of your book. If you're selling hundreds or thousands of copies every month this can add up to a significant amount – easily hundreds or even thousands of dollars a year.

The reason it's a good idea to compress your images is because images are what push your file size up the most, not text. Amazon's recommended compression settings are 50-60%. The advantage of these settings are they reduce the file size significantly (typically by around 75%), but don't compromise the quality of the image too much.

Here is another website, also free, where you can compress your images before you add them into your Word document:

jpeg-optimizer.com

Adding tables

Tables are not supported by Kindle unless you're using the KF8 format.

Including a table in your manuscript this will lead to all sorts of Kindle formatting errors – the table won't resize and will look a real mess. This is despite the fact that tables are very easy to create in Word and work great within your actual Word document.

The simple solution is to create the table you want in a separate document (which you can keep in case you ever need to adjust the table) and then take a screenshot of it so that you, in effect, turn the table into an image. You then insert the image where you want the table to appear in your document. And remember, for tables use GIFs not JPEGs so they display more clearly.

Hyperlinks

A very important feature of Kindle books is that you can add hyperlinks. Hyperlinks allow you to build your list, cross-promote your other books and enhance the experience of your reader by making relevant resources easily available to them.

You've got a choice, you can either hyperlink the URL (the actual address) or you can hyperlink anchor text.

Anchor text is simply text that you have turned into a link. The advantage of anchor text is that it can include a call to action, for example, "Click here to check out Volume 2". Using a call to action, rather than a plain URL, typically increases the likelihood that someone will click the link.

Be aware, however, that if you use anchor text people can't see the underlying URL and, therefore, they can't type the address into a browser. If you're going to have anchor text, I recommend adding a separate link that can be typed as well – in other words, you duplicate the link.

Here's an example of how I've done this with the Crush It with Kindle video series using anchor text ("free video series") for the first link and a shortened (see below) URL for the second:

This book is accompanied by a free video series.

The videos feature additional bonus material that is better suited to video format. They also build on some of the key things covered in the book so watching them will allow you to get as much as you possibly can from the book.

To get instant access to the videos go to **bit.ly/ciwkvideos**

Shortening URLs

URLs can be clicked and typed, but bear in mind that long URLs can lower your click through rate. Firstly, some people are reluctant to click long URLs as it's less clear to them where they'll end up. Secondly, most people simply won't bother typing a URL if it's too long.

The solution is to shorten your URLs. There are various options for this, but the one I use is bitly.com. As well as being free bitly also allows you to track the clicks on your link, which can be very useful. You can track based on the number of clicks, the source of those clicks (e.g., Facebook or Twitter) and which countries they came from.

Adding hyperlinks

How do you actually add hyperlinks?

You've got a choice. The first option is to type the URL or anchor text on to the page, highlight it and then turn that highlighted section into a hyperlink. You do this by right clicking the highlighted section, which opens up a menu on which you click the "Hyperlink" option. This in turn opens up the "Insert Hyperlink" window.

Or you can place your cursor where you want the link to appear, open up the "Insert Hyperlink" window via your toolbar and type the anchor text or URL directly into there.

Within the "Insert Hyperlink" window there are two boxes that need to be filled in. The first is the "Text to display" box. If you have highlighted the text you want to hyperlink it will have already been added. If not then simply type in the URL or anchor text you want shown in your book.

The second box you must complete is the "Address" box. Here you must add the *full* URL including the "http://www..." part as this is where Kindle will send readers when they click the link.

It's very important to test your links before you publish your book. It's so easy to make one little typo and then the link will never work. You don't have to wait until the book is on Kindle to do this; you can test them from within your Word document.

Adding a clickable Table of Contents

I've already mentioned how important it is to have a clickable table of contents (TOC). A clickable TOC dramatically improves your readers' experience by making it much easier to navigate around your book.

As discussed earlier, I recommend going up to three layers deep, but no more – otherwise navigation gets confusing. Of course, you don't have to go that deep if, for example, it makes sense only to use chapter headings (the first layer).

Just to remind you, Heading 1 is for chapters and main sections in the book (if applicable), Heading 2 is for headings within chapters and Heading 3 is for sub-headings.

The table of contents should be at the front of your book. To add your table of contents, the first thing to do is open up a new page in your Word document where you want the TOC to appear. The next step is to click the "References" tab in the toolbar and then click on the "Table of Contents" button. This brings up a drop down menu – now click "Insert Table of Contents" on the menu.

This will bring up a window in which there are three settings you need to adjust to create your table of contents. These are highlighted in the screenshot below:

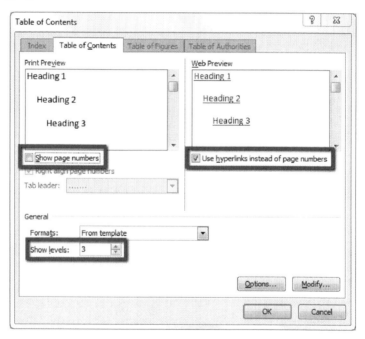

First of all, you need to uncheck the "Show page numbers" box here for the simple reason that reflowable Kindles books don't have page numbers. Once you've done that, check the box to say "Use hyperlinks instead of page numbers".

Finally, select the number of levels you want: either 1, 2 or 3. Once you've done that, click "OK" and you have set up your book's table of contents. The TOC you've just created will automatically link through to the relevant headings within your Word document.

Bookmarking your TOC

Once you've set up your TOC it's important to bookmark it.

Again, this is about improving the experience for your readers. Kindle readers can use the Kindle "Go to..." feature to go directly to certain places in the book, for example, the cover, the beginning and the table of contents. This is very useful for navigating the book quickly.

The cover "bookmark" is set up automatically, Kindle does that for you, but the bookmarks for the beginning of your book and the table of contents are things you have to do yourself.

To bookmark your TOC put the cursor on to the TOC page, click "Insert Tab" on your toolbar and then click the "Bookmark" button. This brings up a window. In the "Bookmark name" box type TOC then click "Add".

That's it! Now people can use the "Go to..." feature on Kindle to navigate directly to your TOC.

Bookmarking the start of your book

Similarly, you may want to bookmark the start of your book. For example, you may have a personal message you want people to read or maybe you have a guide on how to get the most out of your book.

If you do have a page you want to bookmark as the "Start" page then simply follow the same procedure as you did for the table of contents page only instead of typing in TOC you name the bookmark Start with a capital S.

Creating a PDF version of your book

I mentioned earlier that you might want to create a PDF so you have a downloadable version of your book for your website or so that you can send out review copies.

This is very easy to do: simply click on "Save As" and then "PDF". This will bring up a window into which you enter the filename of your book.

Next, using the "Save as type" dropdown menu in the same window select "PDF" and then click the "Publish" button and this will create a PDF of your book.

It's important to note that creating a PDF version is not going to affect your Word document. You'll still have your Word document as well; all this does is create a second version of your document as a PDF file.

That's it!

That's everything you need to do to format your book in Word. Although it might seem like a lot initially, in fact, there aren't that many things that you need to do.

What I suggest is that rather than worrying about trying to remember everything we've gone through, just treat this chapter as a reference guide as and when you need it. You'll find, once you've done one or two books, that the whole process becomes very straightforward.

Part III: Outsourcing your formatting

While formatting your book in Word is pretty straightforward if you still have any concerns, if you want to save time or if you just don't want the hassle then you can outsource it. I'll explain how in a moment, but first I want to mention KF8 (Kindle Fire 8) formatting.

KF8 formatting

According to Amazon, KF8 formatting enables over 150 new formatting options including:

- bullet points
- numbered lists
- tables
- fixed layout pages
- highlighting
- colored text
- drop caps
- Scalable Vector Graphics (graphics that don't lose resolution when magnified)

KF8 also supports HTML5 and CSS3. KF8 formatting can be displayed on the Kindle Fire (as you would expect!), and is being rolled out for newer versions of Kindle and for the Kindle apps. If you upload a KF8 formatted work Amazon will create a second version for displaying on devices that don't support KF8.

If you want your book formatted using KF8 I recommend you outsource the process unless you already have the necessary coding skills. In particular, KF8 is suitable if you are publishing fixed layout books or graphic novels or comics.

Here is the link I gave you earlier to Amazon's KF8 overview page:

www.amazon.com/gp/feature.html?docId=1000729511

Or use this shortened URL: **bit.ly/kf8format**

How to outsource your formatting

The good news when it comes to outsourcing your formatting is that it's both easy and inexpensive. The same freelancer sites that I mentioned earlier are good places to find people to format your books:

- oDesk.com
- Elance.com
- Craigslist
- Fiverr.com

For basic text formatting, I recommend a budget of $5 to $10 per 10,000 words. If the formatting is more complex, for example, you want KF8 formatting or fixed layout pages you will be looking towards the top end of this range – maybe a little bit more. Either way, it's still very cheap: a 50,000 word book will likely cost you around $25 to $50 to format.

This begs the question why even have a chapter about formatting? Why not simply say "Just go ahead and outsource the whole thing"?

Well, the truth is that despite the ease and low cost of outsourcing the process I still format nearly all my books myself. That's because formatting in Word is so easy (once you get used to it) that I simply do it as I go along: I write and format simultaneously.

Then, once the manuscript is finished, I will go back through the whole thing using the Pilcrow feature mentioned earlier to check for formatting errors. This "Pilcrow" check, however, does not add any time to the project as it is something I would be doing anyway – even if I had outsourced the formatting. There's no way I'm going to put a book up on Amazon unless I've checked the formatting personally, even if someone else has done it, and nor should you!

Also, if you are going to outsource effectively you need to know enough about the process to ask the right questions and know whether or not you are getting a good service. So, either way, you still need to know what's involved.

Part IV: Organizing your book

Now that you know how to format your book let's look at how to organize it. This is important because a well-organized book appears more professional – that is to say, more like the sort of books people are used to seeing from traditional publishers.

A professional looking book creates confidence in the minds of your prospective readers and will increase sales. A well-organized book also improves the reader experience.

Broadly speaking, your book should be divided up as follows:
1. Front matter
2. Main text
3. Back matter

Let's look at each of these in turn, starting with the front matter.

Front matter

Here is a list of the front matter that you may want to include in your book. You don't necessarily need all of these items, but if you do include them this is the order in which they would normally appear:
1. Cover (added separately)
2. Title page
3. Copyright page/publishing data
4. Author bio (more often at the back)
5. Dedication
6. Quote (relevant/inspirational)
7. Table of Contents (TOC)
8. Foreword
9. Preface/Introduction

10. Acknowledgements (may be part of back matter)
11. Prologue

The cover does not form part of your manuscript. Your cover file – the file containing the image of your cover – is uploaded separately. Therefore, the first thing that will appear in your manuscript is the title page.

Note that all of these items should start on their own separate pages and be separated by page breaks, as discussed earlier. If you are creating a physical copy of your book they will also normally start on the right hand page (the same goes for chapters), with the exception of the copyright/publishing data page, which is normally on the left.

The next page is the copyright page, which also includes publishing data such as dates of publication, details of the publisher, the ISBN number (if applicable – ISBNs are optional for Kindle as Amazon automatically give you an ASIN number), names of contributors, a disclaimer if you are including one; basically, the key admin information for your book.

Some authors will include their author bio page at the front of their book, though it is more often found at the back. There can be marketing benefits to including it at as part of the front matter if you are trying to position yourself and highlight the products or services you provide. If you do include your author bio in your front matter then it fits most neatly after the copyright page.

After the copyright or author bio page, as the case may be, you normally have the dedication page. Then, if you are including a relevant quote or quotes (inspirational is good, but not a requirement) these go on the following page.

Next, comes your (clickable) table of contents. If somebody has written a foreword for you this follows your table of contents. After the foreword, you put the preface or introduction if you have one.

Next come the acknowledgements, though this is optional. Some authors put the acknowledgements at the front of the book, some at the back. Some authors will include the acknowledgments at the end of their introduction, so that the preface/introduction and acknowledgments are effectively one section. Other authors will have an introduction and then separate acknowledgments. There is an argument for putting them at the back in a Kindle book to allow people using the "Look Inside" feature to see more of your content and get to it faster, but really it's up to you – do whatever you feel is best.

Finally, if your book has a prologue this is the last thing to come before the main body of text.

Back matter

As with the front matter, you may not necessarily need all these items, but this is the order in which they would normally appear:

1. Appendices
2. Glossary
3. Acknowledgements (if not at front)
4. Endnotes (if not using footnotes)
5. Bibliography
6. Index: currently not recommended for Kindle
7. CTAs
8. Author bio (if not at the front)

(Note that 7 and 8 are interchangeable.)

First of all should come any appendixes, followed by a glossary if appropriate. If you decide to put the acknowledgments at the back of your book, rather than the front, then they come next.

You can add footnotes to your book using Word. It is a KDP requirement that footnotes have working links so that the reader can 1) click the footnote link in the main text and go straight to the footnote itself, and then 2) click a link and go straight back to where they were in the main text once they have read the footnote.

To do this, simply add your footnotes in the normal way to your Word document and Amazon will convert them automatically once you upload your file. If you're not familiar with adding footnotes to Word then the steps are outlined here:

kdp.amazon.com/help?topicId=A1IZ6N1F51ZYJ2&ref_=pe_3 90220_117918660_73

Or use this shortened URL: **bit.ly/footnotesword**

In lieu of footnotes you may want to use endnotes, which can either be placed at the end of the relevant chapter or here at the end of the book.

Your bibliography, if you have one, should follow your endnotes. In a printed book the index would come next, however, indexes are not properly supported on Kindle and Amazon does not recommend them.

Integrating back matter with your CTAs

In the previous chapter we talked about the importance of including Calls to Action (CTAs) in your book. These included the "Buy my next book CTA" and the "Review request CTA", both of which would normally come towards the end of your book.

If you have little or no back matter then it's easy to slot your CTAs in at the end of the main text of your book – the ideal spot from your point of view. However, if you have back matter that needs to be included then it's important to bear in mind your readers' experience.

Back matter exists, primarily, because it is useful to readers and helps them get the most from the book. Convention and convenience mean the back matter appears after the main text, but that doesn't make it any less part of the book.

For this reason I recommend adding your CTAs after the other back matter items, with the exception of your author bio. CTAs are, by their very nature, self-serving – even if they also happen to be useful to your readers. Placing them ahead of the other back matter is, therefore, likely to diminish your readers' overall experience and hence the goodwill they have towards you.

Finally, you can include an author bio (if it's not at the front) and contact details together with information about services you offer such as coaching or speaking, links to your websites and social media links.

Note that this could just as easily go before (or between) your CTAs. The order you choose will depend on your most important outcome as whichever item comes first will be seen by the largest number of people.

Is it more important to let people know who you are and what you do or would you rather encourage people to buy your next book or leave a review? Think about how you plan to monetize your book when you are making this decision, but don't agonize over it too much – remember, you can always change your mind and update your manuscript accordingly.

Chapter 6:
Publishing your book

The good news is that Amazon has made the publishing process very straightforward. This chapter takes you through the process step-by-step. You'll find that most of it is pretty intuitive, but there are one or two things to watch out for and I will flag those as we go through the relevant steps in the process.

Your KDP account

Kindle books are published through Amazon's KDP or Kindle Direct Publishing platform. If you have an Amazon account, and I'm guessing you do, you're already enrolled for KDP – as I said earlier, Amazon is very keen to get new content in its race for market share!

The KDP terms and conditions clearly state that you are only allowed to have one KDP account. However, if you are publishing through a company or some other corporate vehicle you will be able to set up a separate KDP account in the name of the company.

To access your KDP account simply go to the KDP home page and login using your Amazon account details:

kdp.amazon.com

Your KDP Bookshelf

Once you're logged into KDP, click on the "Bookshelf" button (top left). Your KDP Bookshelf is where you go to publish and then manage your books. To add a book simply click the "Add new title" button and you will be able to begin the submission process.

There are 10 main steps to publishing your book and you are taken through a two page setup wizard to complete them. Steps 1 to 6 cover the details of the book, while steps 7 to 10 cover book rights, royalties and pricing.

In addition to the 10 main steps you will need to decide whether you want to enroll your book in Amazon's KDP Select program (this is the first thing you will be asked) and you will have to confirm your distribution rights.

KDP Select

KDP Select is an optional program with clear pros and cons (which I'll cover in a moment). Membership of KDP Select is on a book by book basis so just because one book is enrolled in KDP Select it doesn't mean your others have to be. Enrolment is for 90 day blocks so you can enroll a book and then opt-out later.

In most cases I recommend enrolling in KDP Select when you first publish your book as there are some big advantages when it comes time to do your book launch (the subject of chapter 9). Whether you keep your book in KDP Select beyond the first 90 day enrolment period will depend on your long-term objectives (see chapter 10).

The advantages of KDP Select

The primary advantage of KDP Select is that during each enrolment period you're allowed to run one of two types of Amazon promotion for you book. Note that these promotions are offered on an "either or" basis: if you run one type of promo you cannot then run the other within that 90 day enrolment period (though you could do so during the following period).

i) Kindle Free Book Deal

The first type of promotion is the Kindle Free Book Deal (which I'll refer to as the Kindle Free promo) and if you choose this option you're allowed to promote your book for free for up to 5 days in every 90 day period. These 5 days can be done in a single block or split up over the course of the 90 days.

We'll cover exactly why you might want to give your book away for free in detail in chapter 9, as well as how to set up and run a free promotion. However, if you want more information in the meantime here is the link to Amazon's Free Book Promotions FAQ page:

kdp.amazon.com/help?topicId=A34IQ0W14ZKXM9

Or use this shortened URL: **bit.ly/freefaq**

ii) Kindle Countdown

The second promotion option is the Kindle Countdown, which allows you to offer your book at a discount for anywhere between one hour and 7 days.

Note that, unlike the Kindle Free promo where you can split your 5 day allowance up, you are not allowed to run more than one Kindle Countdown in any 90 day enrolment period. So if you run a one hour Kindle Countdown that's it – you don't get to use the rest of your 7 days!

When you run a Kindle Countdown you can choose to vary the level of discount as the "countdown" progresses (you're allowed up to 5 different price increments). By *decreasing* the level of discount as the promo progresses you incentivize people to buy the book sooner rather than later. This is possible because Amazon shows people all the relevant information on the book's page as you can see in this screenshot:

As well as the normal price, both the current (discounted) price and the price that the book will go up to are displayed plus there is a ticking countdown timer that shows you exactly when the price will go up – hence the name of the promotion.

Of course, you can vary your price at any time, but an advantage of Kindle Countdown is that if your book is in the 70% royalty bracket you will still earn that royalty rate even if your book's price falls below $2.99 during the promotion (when normally the royalty would drop to 35%).

Currently Kindle Countdown is only available on Amazon.com and Amazon.co.uk. Plus there are certain eligibility criteria. The most important of these to bear in mind when planning a promotion are that your book must have been in KDP Select for at least 30 days and the price must not have changed for 30 days.

For more information here is a link to Amazon's Kindle Countdown overview page:

kdp.amazon.com/help?topicId=A3288N75MH14B8

Or use this shortened URL: **bit.ly/kcoverview**

And here is a link to Amazon's Kindle Countdown FAQ page:

kdp.amazon.com/help?topicId=A2MJTCAYTCBNW2

Or use this shortened URL: **bit.ly/kcfaqs**

We'll come back to Kindle Countdowns again in chapter 9 when we look at how to set them up and how best to run your campaigns.

iii) Kindle Owners' Lending Library

Another advantage of KDP Select is that you can lend through the Kindle Owners' Lending Library (KOLL). This is a benefit that's available to Amazon Prime users and it allows them to borrow your book for free. The good news, however, is that even though they get it for free you still get paid for it!

Typically, Amazon pays around $2 per borrow, though it varies from month to month as the exact amount is based on the total number of borrows, which is divided into a variable monthly fund.

If your book is part of KOLL you will, of course, get people borrowing it for free who wouldn't otherwise have bought it so KOLL is a way of generating extra royalties. These royalties can be significant and as the price of your book goes up so will the ratio of borrows to sales.

KOLL is also a great way to increase the number of people exposed to your content, books, email list and backend products or services. Since the number of monthly borrows can be significant this benefit should not be underestimated.

Note that books in KDP Select are automatically part of KOLL.

The disadvantage of KDP Select

There is one key disadvantage of KDP Select, which is that your book can't be available digitally anywhere else while it's enrolled in KDP Select.

You are literally giving Amazon exclusive rights to sell and distribute the digital version of your book. To be more precise no more than 10% of the content of your book can be available in digital form elsewhere – for example in the form of blog posts or sample chapters online. This means that you don't even have the right to sell (or give away) your book on your own website – the only way you could do it is via a link to your book's Amazon page.

Note that these restrictions apply only to the digital version of your book not to any physical versions if you have them.

Enrolling in KDP Select

If you want to enroll your book in KDP Select, it's very easy. From within your KDP Bookshelf select the book's "Edit Book Details" page. Once there you will see, at the top of the page, a box entitled "Introducing KDP Select". Just check the radio button that says "Enroll this book in KDP Select" and you're enrolled.

Opting-out of KDP Select

If you wish to distribute the digital version of your book more widely (something we'll be covering in chapter 10) then you will have to opt-out of KDP Select.

This requires opting-out before the current 90 day period ends otherwise your book will be automatically re-enrolled for another full 90 days.

To do this, go to your KDP Bookshelf and select "Edit Book Details" for the relevant book. On the next page click on "Enrolment Details" and a pop-up window will appear. Uncheck the automatic renewal radio button in the pop-up window, hit "Save" and you're done. Note that your book will stay enrolled in KDP Select until the current period ends.

Steps 1 to 6 of the publication process: book details

Once you've decided whether or not to enroll your book in KDP Select you can go on to actually publish it. The first 6 of the steps all relate to the details of your book and are set out in order below:

Step 1: Enter your book details

There are a number of fields to fill in under step 1 as follows:

First of all you must enter the name of your book. You should enter the exact title of your book – you are not allowed to add keywords or extra information.

In the next box you should enter the sub-title of your book. While this is optional I always recommend adding a sub-title whether you are writing fiction or non-fiction. Not only does it allow you to include keywords that make it easier for people to find you book, a good sub-title is also an important way of hooking in potential readers and getting them to want to buy your book.

Next there is a radio button that you check if the book is part of a series. If applicable you should definitely check this because it allows Amazon to cross promote the books in the rest of your series for you.

Underneath this you can enter an edition number. If you're publishing the book for the first time, you can leave this box blank or just put in the numeral 1. If the book has been published before and this version contains significant changes you should put in the appropriate edition number.

Also optional, the next box is for the name of the publisher. If you are self-publishing enter your own name; if you are using a publishing company enter that. You can, if you prefer, leave this blank.

The next box is very important – it's for your description. Getting this right is one of the keys to the success of your book. In chapter 7 I will explain in detail how to create your description and how to use Amazon HTML to show it off as effectively as possible. In the meantime, just be aware that all you have to do once your description is typed up and ready to go is copy and paste it into the box.

Under the description box you have a button that says "Add contributors". You must add at least one contributor for your book, which normally would be the author. However, if necessary you can add multiple contributors such as co-authors, editors, illustrators and translators.

Next you enter the primary language that the book is written in. Following this you have the option to add the "Publication date". If the book has been published previously, you can put that date in. If you're publishing it for the first time you can leave it blank and Amazon will put in the publication date for you automatically.

Finally, if you have an ISBN (International Standard Book Number) you can enter it here. As I explained earlier, you don't need an ISBN as Amazon will automatically assign you an ASIN or Amazon Standard Identification Number.

Note that if you do enter an ISBN it should be unique to the Kindle version of your book: the idea behind ISBNs being that there is a different ISBN for each version of your book.

Step 2: Verify your publishing rights

You have two options here: either your book is a public domain work or it is not public domain and you hold the necessary publishing rights.

There are some important things to mention here: Amazon accepts public domain work, but only subject to some strict criteria. What

Amazon does not allow is content that is "freely available on the web" such as PLR or Private Label Rights material.

Public domain work – such as a book that is now out of copyright – may be published, but only if it has been differentiated. Amazon define three ways of "differentiating" content as follows:

1. **Translated:** A *unique* translation.

2. **Annotated:** An annotated version with annotations that are "…unique, handcrafted, additional content, including study guides, literary critiques, detailed biographies or detailed historical context".

   The italicized words are Amazon's, not mine. Note the use of the word "detailed" – they don't want people trying to get away with just a few lines of annotations. They want genuine, original content that actually enhances the reader's experience of that book.

3. **Illustrated:** An illustrated version that includes "10 or more unique illustrations relevant to the book".

Even if differentiated, books that are entirely or primarily public domain works are not eligible for 70% royalties, nor can they be part of KDP Select.

This KDP Select restriction also applies to works to which others have publishing rights. So let's say you have publishing rights in one territory but somebody else has the publishing rights in another territory then that book *cannot* be Part of KDP Select.

For more information on publishing public domain work visit:

kdp.amazon.com/help?topicId=200743940

Or use this shortened URL: **bit.ly/publicdom**

Having explained all of that, the verification process itself is very simple. You just check the appropriate radio button to say either that it is a public domain work or that it is not public domain and you have the necessary publishing rights.

Step 3: Target your book to customers

This is where you set up your book's categories and keywords. Amazon allows you to add two categories and seven keywords to help customers find your book. I want to stress how important it is to *always use both categories as well as all seven keywords*: you can never have too many ways for people to find your book. I will be covering category and keyword selection in detail in chapter 7, but this where you enter them.

Step 4: Upload or create a book cover

You have a choice of either uploading your own cover design or creating a book cover using the Cover Creator that Amazon has built into this step of the publishing process.

At the time of writing Amazon's Cover Creator is extremely basic and I would not recommend using it at all. I will cover in detail how to get an effective and professional looking cover designed at a reasonable cost in chapter 7. Once you have your cover image ready this is where you upload it.

The uploading process can take several seconds, but once it's finished an image of your cover will be displayed together with the message "Cover uploaded successfully" in green.

Step 5: Upload your book file

This is it – the moment you actually upload the book file itself!

Before you to this you are asked whether or not you want to enable Digital Rights Management – I recommend you don't. That's because having Digital Rights Management in place can create problems for you if and when you start distributing your book outside of Kindle.

The reality is that having Digital Rights Management in place does little to protect your book – people can still rip it off – but may cause you problems if you are distributing your book outside Amazon. In my opinion, it's just not worth the hassle. Note that whatever you decide, once you've made and saved your selection it can't be changed.

Once you've done this you can click the "Browse" button to select your book file and upload it to KDP. This may take some time, particularly if you are uploading a large file, but once it's complete you'll see a message saying "Upload and conversion successful" in green. Underneath this you will be told if there are any likely spelling errors and given a chance to correct them.

Step 6: Preview your book

Once you've successfully uploaded your book file you will be able to go on to step 6, which is to preview your book.

This step is absolutely crucial. As well as the various types of Kindle, your book may be read on tablets, smartphones, Macs or PCs. All of these display slightly differently so it's important to preview the formatting on as many devices as you can to make sure it works.

To check how the book will look on Kindle, Kindle Fire, Kindle Fire HD, Kindle Paperwhite, iPad and iPhone you will need to use the "Online Previewer", which is built into step 6.

To preview the book for Kindle Touch and Kindle DX you will need the "Downloadable Previewer" which is available for download when you reach step 6.

No mention is made of either previewer working for Android tablets or smartphones or for Macs or PCs so I contacted the KDP support team (who are normally very responsive and helpful, by the way) about this. They explained that currently the Kindle previewers do not support these formats.

There is a workaround for Macs and PCs and that is to use the Downloadable Previewer to create a Downloadable Book Preview File, which you can then review using the Kindle app. Clearly this is not ideal as you may not have easy access to these devices. Nor does this cover us for Android tablets or smartphones, however, if your book is correctly formatted for the numerous other devices that are supported then it is likely to be correctly formatted for Android too.

With so many versions to check, this preview process obviously has the potential to be quite time consuming. So just to be clear, this is a rapid preview of your book for any obvious formatting errors, not a proofreading exercise.

For at least one version it's a good idea to scan through every page of the book just to make sure there are no silly formatting errors that you previously missed, but which jump out to you as soon as you see the book in Kindle format rather than Word.

If you need to make corrections to your original manuscript as a result do so and then simply upload the revised version, which will automatically replace the previous one.

You don't need to scan every page of every version – just make sure there is one that you've checked fully and are happy with. Having done this you can then look at the other different versions previewing just the key pages where formatting errors can easily creep in such as the title page, contents page and so on, together with few pages of the main text to make sure that also looks OK.

Save and Continue

Once you're happy with your previewed book click the "Save and Continue" button. This will allow you to progress on to the second of the two pages in the publication process.

Steps 7 to 10 of the publication process: rights, royalties and pricing

Page two of the publication process takes you through steps 7 to 10 – rights, royalties and pricing:

Step 7: Verify your publishing territories

If you are publishing your own book – and assuming you haven't given any territory rights away – then you will have "Worldwide rights" and should check the appropriate radio button.

If for some reason you are publishing a book to which you only have rights in certain territories then check the "Individual territories" radio button and then select the territories to which you have rights from the list below.

Step 8: Choose your royalty

As discussed in chapter 2 you can choose either a 35% royalty or a 70% royalty for each of your books. If you want the 70% royalty then your book must be priced between $2.99 and $9.99 or the equivalent local currency amount for sales on Amazon sites other than Amazon.com. Either side of these prices your book will earn 35% royalties.

Note that it is possible to price your book within the $2.99 and $9.99 price range and yet still select the 35% royalty. The only benefit to doing this is that it allows you to opt-out of Kindle Book Lending (see step 10). To be frank, being able to opt-out isn't much of a benefit so if your book is priced appropriately I would recommend sticking with the 70% royalty.

Factoring in sales tax

You will need to set the prices for each territory your book will be sold in. Something to bear in mind is that EU countries charge a 3% sales tax. The EU countries that Amazon currently has sites for are

123

the UK, Germany, France, Italy and Spain. The reason I mention this is that if you want to display a retail price such as £4.99, then you will need to factor in this sales tax.

To calculate what list price you should enter simply divide the retail price you want by 1.03. So, for example, if I want a retail price of £4.99 then I do the following calculation:

$$4.99/1.03 = 4.84$$

This tells me that the list price I need to enter for Amazon.co.uk is £4.84. When the book goes on sale Amazon will add the 3% sales tax on to the £4.84 and what customers will see is a retail price of £4.99.

Something else to mention is that KDP allows you to do automatic pricing based on the US list price of the book, which you can do simply by checking the radio button for each territory you want this to happen for.

I'm going to recommend you don't do this because it can lead to some really odd prices being displayed. Because Amazon does the currency conversion based on the exchange rate on the day you set your price you could end up with any odd number in there. Yet we know that books with a price ending in .97 or .99 normally sell better. So, by all means use this feature to guide you as to the approximate price you should be charging, but then set the prices up manually with a more marketing friendly suffix.

Step 9: Kindle MatchBook

The Kindle MatchBook program gives customers who buy or have previously bought the print version of your book (if you have one) from Amazon the option to purchase the Kindle version at a promotional price of $2.99, $1.99, $0.99 or free.

Note that the "promotional price" you select must be at least 50% less than the normal price of your Kindle book.

Enrolling your book in Kindle MatchBook will generate some extra sales – albeit at a lower price point and in relatively small numbers. Perhaps more importantly, it will create goodwill with customers who have bought the physical version of your book. Since it only applies to customers who have already bought the physical book through Amazon it is likely to have little, if any, adverse effect on your overall Kindle sales.

Step 10: Kindle Book Lending

The first thing to note is that Kindle Book Lending is not the same as the Kindle Owners' Lending Library (KOLL), which I talked about earlier. KOLL is a service for Amazon Prime members who can borrow your book for free if it is enrolled in KDP Select. Note that with KOLL although Prime members get your book for free you still get paid by Amazon.

With Kindle Book Lending, however, you don't get paid. Kindle Book Lending is a service whereby anyone who has bought a copy of your book is allowed to "lend" their digital copy once and for up to 14 days.

Amazon automatically enrolls all books into the Kindle Book Lending; however, if your book royalty is set at 35% you're allowed to opt-out. If your royalty is set at 70% you don't get that option.

I would recommend allowing Kindle Book Lending even if your book royalty is 35%. Apart from the goodwill it generates, it's another way of introducing new people to your work. That means getting your message out to a wider audience and having more people opting-in to your email list.

Plus, if the borrower likes your book they may decide to buy a personal copy (it will not be available to them once the 14 days is up) or they may decide to buy other books that you have written. Remember, at the end of your book they will be able to click straight through to buy your other books.

Save and publish

Once you've completed steps 1 to 10 you're ready to publish!

If you're happy with everything check the box to confirm your publishing rights and compliance with Amazon's terms and then click the "Save and Publish" button.

You will then get a confirmation message to let you know your book has been saved and that the publishing process is underway. It usually takes between 12 and 24 hours for your book to go live on Kindle. Once it is live you will get an email from Amazon letting you know and with a link to your book's page – happy days!

This isn't quite the end of the process though. It's very important that once your book is live you actually review it.

Review your (live) book

As soon as Amazon notifies you that your book is live I recommend you go straight to the book's page to make sure everything is correct. Check your cover image, title, sub-title, book description and editorial reviews (covered in chapter 7) to make sure all these vital elements are correct and displaying the way they should.

Then there's the book itself. Yes, you've checked it using the Kindle previewers, but (since I'm sure you'll want a copy of your own book anyway) buy it and scan through it again to check the formatting is correct – formatting really does matters to the long-term success of your book so this one last check is worth doing.

Editing your book after publishing

If you need to correct an error, or if you ever wish to edit your book after publishing it, doing so is very simple. Simply go to your KDP Bookshelf and under the heading "Other Book Actions" select either "Edit Book Details" (steps 1 to 6) or "Edit Rights, Royalty and Pricing" (steps 7 to 10).

Once you're on the page you want just follow the relevant steps covered above to make your changes. If you've edited the text of the book you will need to upload the file containing the revised manuscript, which will automatically replace the previous version. The same applies if you are changing your cover image.

Once you've completed your edits confirm your rights and click "Save and Publish" as before. The new version will typically go live in 12 to 24 hours and you will be notified by email when it does.

As far as the public are concerned there is no interruption in service: the existing version of your book remains available until Amazon has processed the new version at which point there is a seamless switchover.

Note that before publishing an edited version of your book it is a good idea to check it again with the Kindle previewers. Unfortunately, it's very easy for formatting errors too creep in unnoticed.

Chapter 7:
Building a bestseller

We've covered a lot in the last six chapters: the incredible opportunity that Kindle publishing gives us; how to monetize your book; how to choose a profitable niche or genre; how to write your book quickly; how to format your book; and, how to publish your book. Having a published book is great, but it doesn't matter how good it is unless people know about it: until they do you won't make any sales.

Chapters 7, 8, 9 and 10 are all about marketing your book so that you can maximize both the sales and the impact of your book. There are three distinct phases to marketing your book and these phases are covered over the course of the next four chapters.

The first phase, which we'll be covering here in chapter 7, is all about getting the foundations right. There are certain things that need to be correctly in place, without which your book is unlikely to succeed. On the other hand, get these things right and every one of your future marketing efforts will be much more successful – that's why I've entitled this chapter "Building a bestseller".

The second phase is your book's launch. This is when we put together a launch campaign that will rocket your book up the bestseller lists as well as getting it properly positioned on Amazon for long-term success. We'll cover how to get Amazon to promote your book for you and why it's so important in chapter 8 and then in chapter 9 we'll look at how to actually launch your book so that it rocket's up the bestseller lists.

The third phase is any ongoing marketing of your book that you choose to do once the launch phase is over. We'll cover that in chapter 10.

Amazon's BIG SECRET

I'm going to let you in on Amazon's BIG SECRET. Whatever you do, don't share this information! ;-) And here it is...

It's way easier to get a #1 bestseller on Amazon than most people ever imagine. You see Amazon has so many categories and sub-categories you can get to #1 with a very small number of sales. In fact, it's not uncommon for people to hit #1 status in some of the less competitive sub-categories with less than a hundred sales.

Of course, I'm going to teach you how to sell a lot more than a hundred books!

Do bear in mind that however many books you sell there is no guarantee you'll get to #1. You might be unlucky and launch your book only to find that you're up against the year's big blockbuster in your niche or a book that has a much bigger marketing budget behind it than yours. But, with the right foundations for your book and a great launch you've got a very good chance.

The 9 steps to building a bestseller

Here are the 9 steps to building a Kindle bestseller (i.e., getting those foundations in place) in the order we'll be covering them:

1. Keyword research
2. An attention grabbing title
3. A powerful sub-title
4. A cover that "pops"
5. The right Amazon categories
6. A great description

7. Amazon HTML
8. Social proof: customer reviews
9. Social proof: editorial reviews

What all of these elements do is lead your prospect through the process that they need to follow before they buy a book. Getting these 9 steps right dramatically increases the likelihood that someone who sees your book will actually buy it.

Think of book buying as a linear process. First of all your cover has to grab someone's attention amongst all the other competing cover thumbnails on the Amazon page (or books on the bookstore shelf). Next the title must interest the prospect enough for them to want to find out more about the book. The sub-title (always have a sub-title!) builds their interest levels and gets them checking out either the description or the book itself.

At this stage people will typically read (or skim) the description, look at the contents page if you have one, check out the first few pages of the book and look at a few reviews. All these things taken together must be enough to convince them to buy the book.

If there is a "breakdown" at any stage of this linear process then it's game over – you've lost the sale. That's why getting these foundations right is so important and why they will make such a difference both to ALL of your future marketing efforts and to the number of organic sales made by your book.

Step 1: Keyword research

Although the first thing that usually grabs someone's attention is the cover I've left it until step 4 because before you can design your cover you need to know what the title (and sub-title) of your book will be.

Keyword research is an essential pre-requisite to choosing your title and sub-title, hence it's here at step 1. If you're not familiar with keyword research here's a quick explanation of what it is and why it's important.

Keywords are the words or phrases people type in when they want to find something either through a search engine or on a specific website. When you publish your book you want people to be able to find it, and not just on Amazon. You also want them to be able to find it if they are searching on Google as well – this is something that can drive a lot of sales. You do this by including keywords in the title and/or subtitle of your book.

Amazon also allows you to enter up to 7 keywords or keyword phrases when publish your book on KDP; this is during step 3 of the publishing process that we covered in chapter 6. These keywords are not seen by the general public, but are there to help Amazon to know what your book is about so they can put it in front of the right customers.

So, in order for the right people to find your book you need to discover what they are searching for and that process is what we call keyword research. The good news is that you have two fantastic keyword research tools at your disposal and both of them are free!

The first of these is the Google keyword planner – formerly known as the Google keyword tool:

adwords.google.com/KeywordPlanner

Or use this shortened URL: **bit.ly/gkwp**

You will need to sign up for a Google Adwords account to be able to use it, though this will not cost you anything. The second tool is the dropdown menu built into the search feature in Amazon's Kindle store (which I'll refer to as the "Kindle store search").

Both keyword research tools have different advantages and you will get the best results by using them both. The Google keyword planner is great for generating ideas, plus it shows you how many people are searching for that term each month on Google, allowing you to gauge its popularity. The Kindle store search is great because it shows you exactly what phrases people are searching for on Kindle. It also shows them in order of popularity, although it does not give you the actual number of searches.

Bear in mind that the search results you get are "context dependent". What I mean by this is that, broadly speaking, people use Google and Amazon for different types of searches. Google is somewhere people search for information, whereas Amazon is somewhere people search to buy books. Therefore it is not necessarily the case that a search that is very popular on Google will be similarly popular on Amazon (and vice versa). If in doubt remember that Amazon is where your buyers are and lean towards what people are actually searching for when they are in book buying mode.

First and foremost this keyword research is to help your book get found on Amazon. However, because Amazon is such a high authority site you have a chance of getting your book's Amazon page to rank high on Google as well when people are searching for books on your topic. A high ranking on Google can generate hundreds or even thousands of extra sales.

Using the Google keyword planner

From the Keyword Planner home page click "Search for new keyword and ad group ideas". This takes you onto a page where you can type your keyword ideas (separated by commas) into a search box.

Before making your search you should target it geographically. In my case, over 90% of my book sales are in the US so I target my search accordingly. You can also further target your search by language. Once you've set your search parameters hit the "Get ideas" button and your search results will be returned on the next page. Click the "Keyword ideas" tab to see not only the results for your search terms, but also many (perhaps hundreds) of similar search terms suggested by Google.

These suggested results are what make the Google Keyword Planner so great for generating ideas. I recommend that you shortlist the keyword ideas that you think are most relevant to your target audience, note the number of searches they get, and then cross check them using the Kindle store search feature.

Using Kindle store search

On the left side of the Amazon search bar is a drop down menu that allows you to search different areas of the store. Click on this and select Kindle Store.

You can now type your keyword ideas into the search bar and, as you type, Amazon will display a dropdown list of suggested search terms based on what you are typing. What's so important about these suggestions is that they are not displayed in alphabetical order: *they are displayed in order of their popularity.*

This is huge – not only is Amazon showing you the exact phrases people are searching for within the Kindle store they are also showing you which ones get the most searches.

Now unfortunately there's nothing to tell you the actual number of searches – just the order in which they rank – but this is still great information. Because you don't get the actual number of searches I recommend you do a couple of things to build up the most complete picture you can:

First, do a separate search on Kindle for each of the different keywords on your shortlist and see what comes up. Second, cross-check any promising looking new ideas that are thrown up by your Kindle store search on Google to see what the search volume is like. As you do this bear in mind that, as I said earlier, the volume of searches on Google will not necessarily reflect what is most popular on Amazon as people are typically in different "search modes" on the two sites. Nonetheless, by cross checking the results you get from both sites you will build up a pretty good picture of which keywords are best for your book.

Your KDP 7 keywords

You may remember from step 3 of the publishing process in chapter 6 that you get to choose 7 keywords for your book that you add via your KDP bookshelf. These are not seen by the public, but help Amazon target your book when people are searching.

As well as noting down keyword ideas for your title and sub-title you should be making a shortlist for your 7 KDP keywords. Amazon recommends that you don't duplicate keywords that are already in your title or sub-title because it already uses them to target search results. Think of these as 7 bonus keywords.

Short, medium and long tail keywords

This is not a book on SEO (Search Engine Optimization) so I'll keep things simple. Broadly speaking, we can divide keywords into short tail, medium tail and long tail.

Short tail keywords are words or short phrases that tend to correspond with broad, high level searches. An example might be "weight loss" for which, at the time of writing, there were 110,000 searches a month on Google.

Long tail keywords are longer, more specific phrases. Staying in the weight loss category an example would be "Chinese green tea weight loss" for which there are currently only 170 searches a month on Google.

Somewhere in between our two examples we have "green tea weight loss". This is less specific than our last example, but much more specific than the first: something that is reflected in the number of searches at 14,800 a month.

There are pros and cons to using short or long tailed keywords in your book title. Short tail keywords are much more competitive and harder to rank for. They also convert (to sales) less well because they are more general. On the other hand lots of people are using them to search.

Long tail keywords, on the other hand, are much easier to rank for and they convert better. Of course, the flip side is that because they are much more specific fewer people are using them to search.

Now having said this, it's a lot easier to rank for short tail keywords on Amazon than on Google. That's because on Amazon you are only competing against the other books on Kindle – most of which will not be targeting the same keywords as you. You may still be competing against hundreds of books, but this is nothing compared to the millions of web pages on Google.

On Google, then, it will be very hard to rank anywhere meaningful for these highly competitive phrases, but that's OK and to be expected – the reason they're important to us is because they still have tremendous and ranking potential on Amazon. That's why it's definitely worth including some short tail keywords either in your title and/or your sub-title (more on where to place your keywords in steps 2 and 3 of this chapter).

You will usually find that it's possible to combine a variety of short, medium and long tail keywords in your title and sub-title. Let's look at an example of how this might be done:

Suppose you're considering the title "Chinese Green Tea for Weight Loss". That's a title that includes the following keywords with the monthly search numbers in brackets:
- weight loss (110,000)
- green tea (90,500)
- green tea weight loss (14,800)
- Chinese green tea (1,300)

- Chinese green tea weight loss (170)

That's two short tail, one medium tail and two long tail keywords in our title ("green tea" is short tail with around 90,500 monthly searches; "Chinese green tea" is long tail with 1,300 monthly searches).

Some people categorize keywords as short, medium or long based on the number of words in the phrase. While there is a strong correlation between the number of words and search frequency this is not absolute. Case in point: our example above of "green tea weight loss" is four words but gets more than eleven times more searches than the three word phrase "Chinese green tea". In my opinion the most important metric by far is the number of searches.

By the way, there is no set number at which keywords suddenly become short, medium or long tail. Rather, there is a continuum with broad, frequently used search terms at one end and specific infrequently used terms at the other. (Note that the monthly search numbers shown in the Google Keyword Planner are shown for "exact matches" only.)

Now you know how to do the necessary keyword research let's look at how to take your results and use them to craft your title (step 2) and sub-title (step 3).

Step 2: An attention grabbing title

While keyword research is a critical part of creating your title, the title should definitely not be based on keywords alone. Your title has to grab attention: it has to make your book stand out from all the others in the Amazon search results and instantly make people want to find out more about it (otherwise they'll never buy it). Specifically, it must speak to your target market. There's no point attracting people who, once they check it out, will have no interest in buying your book.

I want to stress here that you should never sacrifice a great title for the sake of keywords. If you can't include keywords in your title in a way that reads naturally and works to support the message of your title then don't include them – put them in your sub-title instead.

Think of the last time you browsed through a newspaper. Each article has a headline designed to grab your attention. Did you read the whole paper? No, you skimmed through the headlines and you only read the articles that interested you... based on their headline. Without a good headline the article never gets read. Without a good and targeted title your book will never get bought.

What your title needs to do

From a marketing point of view, a good title has to achieve several different things in just a few words. In a perfect world it will:

- Grab attention
- Speak to your target market
- Create instant understanding of what the book is about
- Be easy to read and remember
- Make an exciting promise or highlight an exciting benefit
- Tell prospects what pain they will avoid (if applicable)
- Tell people something about how it works (if applicable)
- Incorporate the words "you" and "your" (if applicable)

Note that if you can't achieve all of these things in your title (which is quite likely!) don't worry – you can roll things over to your sub-title. It must, however, do the first two things on the list: grab attention and speak to your target market.

Grabbing attention

Your title might grab attention because it's unusual, controversial or outrageous in some way. Or, it might grab attention because it promises a great benefit to your prospect or a solution to a problem they face.

As a general rule the shorter you can make your title and still achieve your objectives the better – shorter titles are easier to read as people scan through search results and therefore more likely to grab their attention.

That said, if you have an amazing title don't sabotage it just for the sake of making it shorter. A good example of a longish, but outstanding title is "The 7 Habits of Highly Effective People" by Stephen R Covey. Since it was published in 1989 it has stayed consistently in the bestseller lists and sold over 25 million copies and the book's name hits all the appropriate requirements for a great title.

Speak to your target market

In the process of grabbing attention your title can't be too generic – it must contain enough of the right information to be noticed by those readers who will actually want to buy it.

This may seem completely self-evident, but you'd be amazed how many book titles fail to do this. One of the biggest mistakes I see is the use of what I call "cute and clever titles". These are titles that make a cute or clever reference to something (often something obscure) within the book and which make perfect sense to the author who knows their book inside out. However, the reference means nothing to the *prospective* reader who – by definition – has not read the book. For all practical purposes, then, the title is meaningless to the target buyers.

Create instant understanding of what the book is about

This follows on very closely from "speaking to your target market". The more your target market can instantly understand not just that your book is relevant to them, but also why, the more likely they are to be interested in it.

Be easy to read and remember

If you can, try and incorporate the "three Rs" into your title: rhyme, rhythm and repetition (alliteration).

These will make your title both easier to read and easier to remember. This creates a greater sense of understanding, and it's been shown that this increases the likelihood that people will buy it.

Conversely, if a title is hard to read and difficult to understand people will sub-consciously assume (rightly or wrongly) that your book is too and your sales will suffer as a result.

Some classic examples of titles that incorporate some or all of the three Rs are:

- The Cat in the Hat (rhyme, rhythm and repetition)
- The Great Gatsby (rhythm and repetition)
- Pride and Prejudice (rhythm and repetition)
- War of the Worlds (rhythm and repetition)

Your title doesn't have to include all three, but the more it does have the better.

Make an exciting promise

This goes back to grabbing attention. It's not enough to let people know your book is relevant to them. You also need to give them a reason to find out more. And that reason should be something that's exciting to them – either something they will gain (pleasure) or something they will avoid or get rid of (pain).

In the case of fiction and some non-fiction the promise is pleasure: the excitement, intrigue, interest and entertainment they will gain from reading your story or book. Your title must hint at one or more of these things.

Tell prospects what pain they will avoid

In the case of non-fiction "how to" books your title and/or sub-title should highlight both the pleasure they will gain and the pain they will avoid when their problem is solved.

Studies have shown that the avoidance of pain is twice as motivating to people as the pursuit of an unrealized gain so it's important to include both of these elements.

Tell people something about how it works

This is something that can be incorporated into the titles of non-fiction "how to" books. It's optional, but if done properly can go a long way towards persuading people to buy.

"The 7 Habits of Highly Effective People" is a great example of a book that achieves this is. Just by reading the title the prospect understands: 1) the promise of the book – that they will become highly effective; and, 2) how this will be achieved – they will learn 7 habits.

Incorporate the words "you" and "your"

If you are writing a "how to" type book then incorporating the pronouns "you" or "your" in your title can help to create the impression in the mind of your prospect that you are speaking directly to them.

Step 3: A powerful sub-title

You sub-title should be carefully crafted to build on your title. The good news is that your sub-title can be longer than your title and you have more flexibility with it – as long as your title has done its primary job of grabbing the attention of your target market. In fact, without a good title your sub-title is somewhat academic as most people won't read it anyway.

Because your title has to achieve so much in so few words it's unlikely that you will be able to include in it all the keywords you would like. This is where your subtitle comes to the rescue.

A properly crafted sub-title can be very powerful and help you communicate a lot of information. You can use your sub-title to:

- Build on the promise or benefit in your title
- Tell prospects what pain they will avoid
- Further explain what the book's about
- Tell people how the book works
- Overcome objections
- Incorporate the words "you" and "your"
- Create mystery, suspense or intrigue
- Create controversy
- Tell people the book is part of a series or trilogy

As you can see, most of these things build on what you're already trying to achieve with the title. In a moment I'll take you through a worked example of how to craft a title and sub-title that work together to do the things we've discussed. But first, let me touch on the things in this list that weren't covered in the previous step.

Overcome objections

This is something that applies to non-fiction "how to" books. When people read the promise in your title their natural skepticism will kick in. In fact, the bigger and more exciting your promise the more skeptical they are likely to be. Anything you can do to overcome this skepticism will be a big help to your sales.

An example of this would be if you were writing a book on weight loss. One of the first things people will think is that your solution probably involved dieting – and for most people dieting is strongly associated with the pain and discomfort of feeling hungry and struggling with willpower and guilt. Not a good starting point for making sales!

That's why overcoming this objection – if you can do so legitimately – is important. In this case a sub-title that explains that they can achieve their goal "...without dieting" will go a long way towards setting their mind at ease and increasing your likelihood of making the sale.

Tell people if the book is part of a series or trilogy

If your book is part of a series or trilogy then you should make this clear on the cover as communicating this will increase your sales.

Firstly, that's because when people enjoy a book they want to go on to read more. It's a bittersweet feeling to get to the end of a book you've really enjoyed – yes, you had fun reading it, but now it's over. Knowing there is more to read overcomes this feeling and so plays into the psychology of purchasing the book in the first place.

There is also an element of social proof in having a book that is part of a series or trilogy. The more successful something is the more likely it is to be made into a series. People make mental shortcuts when evaluating things (known as heuristics) – this is entirely natural and happens because we have so much information to constantly process. Seeing that your book is part of a series triggers an assumption that other people have enjoyed it enough to merit further volumes.

Worked example: crafting a title and sub-title

Let's return to our "Chinese green tea for weight loss" example and see if we can a) improve the title, and b) craft a suitable sub-title to go with it.

"Chinese green tea for weight loss" may be pretty good as far as keywords are concerned, but as a book title we could do better. For a start it could make a more specific promise.

"Drink Green Tea and Lose Weight" is a much stronger and more specific promise. In order to keep the length down we have had to lose one of our keywords (Chinese), but that's OK as we can bring it back in our sub-title.

So how about a sub-title to build on that? What about this:

"Discover the 7 ancient weight loss secrets of Chinese green tea and the simple system that lets you harness their power to lose weight quickly and easily without dieting."

Now, just to be clear, this sub-title is entirely made up. I have no idea if there are 7 ancient Chinese green tea weight loss secrets. But I bet that if there were a lot of people would want to know what they are and would buy the book! Now let's break that sub-title down.

First of all, notice how long it is. There's no way it would ever get read if it was a title. The only way people will read this is if your title is good enough to hook them first. Then your powerful sub-title can work its magic.

Also, you wouldn't want the sub-title as it appears at the top of your book's Amazon page to be this long – too much text is off-putting. So for the Amazon page you would create a shorter version. However, you could put a longer version like this on the cover of the book itself and at the start of the book's description.

By the way, I'm also presupposing that everything in the sub-title is true. Please don't make stuff up!

Anyway, let's break that sub-title down and analyze it:

"Discover... ancient [Chinese]... secrets"

This creates mystery and intrigue. People love to discover things especially secrets – and even better if it's an ancient secret. And people know that Chinese culture goes back thousands of years and is full of mystery.

"7 ancient weight loss secrets"

Now we're getting specific. People like things that can be broken down into a specific number of items or steps. Odd numbers are better than even and 7 is usually the sweet spot. A top 10 or a top 20 can also work well.

I would recommend that you use the numeral (7) rather than the word (seven). Forget what your English teacher taught you. This is about grabbing attention and selling books – it's not an essay competition. Numerals catch the eye much better.

"weight loss"

This keyword was in our original working title, but not in the final version. See how we got it back in?

"Chinese green tea"

Ditto

"the simple system that lets you harness their power"

Now we're telling people there's a system they can use. This is how the book delivers the results. People love systems – systems can be followed and that makes getting results easier.

Plus, as an extra bonus our system is "simple".

Some useful alternatives to "system" include: stages, strategy, formula, blueprint, framework, habits, rituals, philosophy and lifestyle.

We're also including the pronoun "you" in this phrase. This helps to create the impression in the mind of your prospect that you are speaking directly to them.

"harness their power to lose weight"

We're building on the promise here. Weight loss is what our buyer is interested in and we're implying that there is real power in the secrets and the system (it has to be "harnessed" for heaven's sake – that's what you have to do with horses!).

"simple... quickly and easily"

People love simple, they love quick and they love easy. Always have done, always will.

"without dieting"

This is a big one – it overcomes the number one objection. Dieting is pain. People don't want to buy pain! "Without dieting" tells them that they can get the weight loss benefits without suffering the pain that they normally associate with dieting.

As I mentioned earlier, the avoidance of pain is twice as motivating to people as the pursuit of an unrealized gain (pleasure). So, if you can, you want to address both in your sub-title. Not least because if you don't then people will sub-consciously assume that the pain is there and you're just keeping quiet about it. Use your sub-title to overcome what will otherwise be powerful objections.

Now that's a lot to get through in one sub-title. It doesn't have to be that long, but I wanted to work through a full range of examples with you and show you how powerful a good sub-title can be.

To sum up, it's worth spending some time doing keyword research and crafting your title and sub-title so that they work together to achieve as many of your marketing objectives as possible. The time you spend crafting a good title will pay you back many times over.

Step 4: A cover that "pops"

The job of your cover is not to look pretty. The job of your cover is to sell your book – period. That's not to say it can't look pretty, by the way! Pretty is good as long as it still fulfils its primary purpose of selling your book.

The most important thing to consider when creating your cover is how it first appears to people on Amazon: it appears as a small thumbnail. People won't be able to see your pretty pictures and they probably won't be able to read your sub-title (though it they can it's a bonus). In fact, all they are likely to be able to read – and therefore all you have to draw them in with – is your title. And, of course, the impression created by the cover itself.

Your title should be in large bold lettering so it stands out. I would recommend using all caps because that greatly increases readability. And it should definitely be in a highly contrasting color to the background field so that it stands out clearly.

Bold colors work well for the cover of your book. It's worth spending some time on Amazon looking at search results and noticing which covers grab your attention (and why) as well as which don't. Which colors stand out more amid the many competing thumbnails on the page?

Note that it is OK to use a white background for your cover as long as the title wording and any image that appears on it are bold and striking.

If you are using an image on your cover make sure that it is clear, bold and easy to understand. The right image can be very useful in helping to communicate to prospects what your book is about. Therefore, it's very important that if you use an image it's congruent with the title of your book. Avoid falling into the "cute and clever" trap I talked about earlier – in other words, don't use an obscure image that won't mean anything to prospective readers.

These things will make your book stand out in the search results. They are what will get people clicking on it and prevent it being lost in a sea of competition (the typical Amazon search results page shows at least twenty cover thumbnails).

Crush It with Kindle

Getting your cover designed

There are lots of websites where you can go to get your covers designed and you can pay anything from $5 to several hundred dollars.

A great place to get your cover designed quickly and cheaply is on **fiverr.com** (spelt double r). As the name suggests, on fiverr you can buy services – known as gigs – for just $5. With prices starting so low the quality of what you get can vary tremendously, but some of the work is excellent. And because it's so cheap you can afford to get a number of designs made to test and compare.

Freelance sites like **Elance.com**, **oDesk.com** and **99designs.com** are also good places to find designers. These sites will cost considerably more than fiverr and, of the three, 99designs is likely to be the most expensive.

The good news is it's easy to shop around and compare the work of different designers before you commit.

Cover dimensions

Amazon recommends cover dimensions of 1,563 x 2,500; however, this is not a requirement. I recommend that you consider cover dimensions of *up to* 1,875 × 2,500.

These dimensions will still work on Kindle, but will give you a wider looking cover. This can be an advantage if you have a lot of information that you want to include on your cover without it looking crowded, such as a longish title and sub-title together with an image that supports them. Having a wider cover will also help your thumbnail stand out amongst search results as it will appear slightly bigger on the page.

Just to be clear, I'm not saying that you should have cover dimensions of up to 1,875 × 2,500, but rather that you consider

148

whether these dimensions would work better for the cover your book needs.

Split testing your covers

I strongly recommend split testing your covers before publishing your book. Split testing is easy to do and can have more of an impact on your sales than almost anything else in the marketing process.

Split testing is when you send traffic to two (or more) versions of an ad or web page on which you request the visitor to take a specific action such as clicking the ad or entering an email address. Normally the two versions will be identical except for one variable – that is the variable you are testing.

The best place to split test your covers is on Facebook. The process of setting your ads up is intuitive – just click the "Ads Manager" link in the left hand column of your news feed page and follow the steps as they are presented to you. It's easy to include images and running a campaign is quick and inexpensive.

When you set the ads up be very careful to make sure that all the variables are the same except for the images. It is possible to set one ad up and then upload a variety of images and have Facebook run a different ad for each image. It's also possible to duplicate an existing ad and then simply change the image.

Both of these options are tempting because they save time upfront, but I don't recommend them. That's because Facebook tends to show whichever ads are successful initially without giving the remaining ads a fair chance. This can make it very difficult to get meaningful results. To avoid this problem set your ads up individually and put each ad in a separate ad set.

Because click through rates are low for most Facebook ads I like my ads to be seen by at least 40,000 people (the ad's "Reach") so that I am comfortable that I have enough data on which to make a decision.

Normally I will test around five different cover designs – one of the reasons Fiverr is such an attractive option. I'm happy to test using just basic draft designs as people only see a thumbnail version. Then, once I have a winning design I can spend more getting it worked up so that it appears more professional. For split testing five covers I would budget around $100.

What you need to look for is the click through rate (CTR) for your ads. The actual number is not important; what is important is how the ads perform relative to one another.

During one book marketing project that I did for a client I ran a series of cover split tests for a book that had already been published. After testing several designs I was able to increase in the CTR by 338% compared to the original cover. In other words, *more than three times as many people* were clicking on the book's thumbnail. As you can imagine, this is having a huge impact on sales!

Step 5: The right Amazon categories

Amazon allows you to choose two categories for your book and getting them right is vital. It's vital for getting your book to bestseller status and to give it a chance of hitting #1 bestseller in one or more of its categories. It's also vital if your book is to have long-term sales success.

If you choose a category that's too broad and competitive and it can be very hard to rank well. The more you can niche down into a small, but relevant category the more chance you have of ranking well and of getting to the coveted #1 bestseller slot for your category.

The category mismatch

When you come to publish your first book you will quickly find that the categories you select from in KDP do not match the categories on the Amazon website. This is an ongoing problem of which Amazon is fully aware, but for reasons unknown has yet to be fixed. In other words, we just have to deal with it!

The best way to deal with it is to forget about the categories in KDP, at least while you're doing your category research, and focus on the categories in Amazon's Kindle store under the heading eBooks. The reason for this is simple: you want to base your chosen categories on what your customers will see and be basing their own book searches on.

Note that the categories in Amazon's book store are slightly different from the categories in Amazon's Kindle eBook store, therefore it's very important that you base your searches on the Kindle eBook store categories.

How Kindle categories are arranged

Each Kindle category and sub-category has its own bestseller list (the top 100 books in that category). Since your book is likely to be in multiple sub-categories it will have multiple chances of becoming a bestseller.

We covered how Amazon organizes its Kindle bestseller lists near the start of chapter 3, however, here is a recap:

1. First of all there is the overall bestseller list – the top 100 books on Kindle.
2. Next you have the bestseller lists for fiction and non-fiction. Again, as with all Amazon's bestseller lists, we are talking about the top 100 books in each case.
3. Below this you have Amazon's top level categories, which will sit underneath either fiction or non-fiction. At the time of writing there are 27 top level categories on Amazon.com,

though both the number of categories and the categories themselves vary from time to time. Each top-level category has its own bestseller list.

4. Finally, underneath the top-level categories there are various sub-categories. There may be several sub-categories underneath a particular top-level category, with each sub-category having its own bestseller list.

Kindle has lots of categories and they change surprisingly often. You are allowed to choose two for your book and the best way to do it is to think from the point of view of your prospective customer.

Go to the Kindle book store and look through the categories and sub-categories that are there. Look as well at the sort of books that are showing up when you click on those categories.

Another way of getting ideas for your categories is to look up existing books that are similar to yours and see which categories they are in. You will find this information in the "Product Details" section of the book's page, though the category hierarchy will only be displayed if the book is a bestseller in at least one of its categories or sub-categories.

Think as well about choosing two distinct top level categories if both can apply to your book (remember, Kindle has around 27 top level categories (covering fiction and non-fiction) under which all the various sub-categories are nestled). By having two different top level categories your book gets exposure to a wider audience. If you choose two (sub-) categories that are both within the same top level category its exposure will be more limited.

When to choose different top level categories

An example of a book that could happily live in two distinct top level categories would be a book on time management. People

search for books on time management within both personal
development and business, for example:

> > Business & investing > Management & leadership >
> **Leadership**

> > Advice & how to > Self-help > **Personal transformation**

The categories you would actually select I have put in bold: 1)
Leadership and 2) Personal transformation. The advantage to
choosing these sub-categories is that our book can now be found by
two different audiences searching within two distinct top level
categories.

When to stay with one top level category

However, this won't always be possible – or at least advisable.
Going back to our "Drink Green Tea and Lose Weight" example, it
would be very difficult to find two suitable top level categories from
Amazon's current list. And given the lack of suitable alternatives it
would probably not be advisable. The options I would choose for
this are:

> > Advice & how to > Diets & weight loss > Diets > ? (see
> below)

> > Advice & how to > Health, mind & body > Nutrition

As you can see, both come under the "Advice and how to" main
category. This is not the end of the world though, as both the sub-
categories get a lot of traffic.

Choosing from different sub-categories options

Underneath the Diets sub-category there are, at the time of writing,
four further sub-categories:

> > Healthy

> > Low Fat

> Weight Loss

> Weight Maintenance

And if you know anything about green tea, you'll know that you could legitimately fit this book into any one of those sub-categories. So how do you decide which is sub-category to place your book in?

Calculating a category's competitiveness

The answer is that you will have to do a little bit of research into your sub-category options. You're looking for what I call an "easy top 10" category. This is a category in which your book can rank in the top 10 with relatively few sales. The reason this is so important is that a top 10 ranking means that your book is easily visible to anyone searching within that category. This visibility will generate sales and those sales will help keep your book in the top 10, creating a virtuous circle that promotes long-term organic sales.

Amazon uses a moving average with a strong recency bias to calculate its bestseller lists, which are updated on an hourly basis. Therefore, the exact number of sales that will keep your book in the top 10 of any given category will be constantly changing. As a rough guide, however, the following numbers will help you calculate a category's competitiveness:

Kindle top #10,000 = $\geq$ **10 copies sold per day**

Kindle top #20,000 = $\geq$ **5 copies sold per day**

In other words, for your book to be ranking in the top 10,000 books on Kindle it will need sales of around 10 or more copies per day. To be ranking in the top 20,000 on Kindle it will need sales of around 5 or more copies per day. Knowing these numbers allows you to quickly check whether or not a possible category is an "easy top 10" category.

I've given you these numbers, by the way, because they are very achievable if you have a well written book that is properly marketed. For a more comprehensive guide to estimating daily sales based on Kindle sales rank see the table below.

Let me give you an example of how I do this so that it makes more sense. To analyze a category I will look at the 1st, 5th and 10th ranked books in that category to see where they rank overall on Kindle. Taking these in reverse order I might get something like the following:

Let's say that the 10th ranked book in my target category has an overall Kindle rank of 25,000. This tells me that if my book sells five or more copies a day it will be able to rank in the top 10 for that category.

Next let's say that the 5th ranked book has an overall Kindle rank of 15,000. This tells me that if I my book sells ten or more copies a day it should comfortably rank in the top five for that category.

Finally, let's say that the top ranked book in that category as an overall Kindle rank of 5,000. This tells me that ranking #1 in that category will take a bit more work. In fact, by checking the sales rank chart below I can see that my book would need to sell around thirty copies a day to hit the number one spot. This is easily achievable if I'm running a campaign to promote the book, though it will be harder to maintain for the long-term.

Of course, this is just a snapshot – an hour in the life of the top 10 for that category. Nonetheless, these snapshots give you a pretty good picture of what it will take to rank in the top 10 of any given category, although I do recommend you check the figures once a day for two or three days before making a final decision.

Kindle sales rank chart

This chart shows the approximate number of daily sales you can expect a Kindle book to be making based on its overall Kindle sales rank. As well as using it to check category competitiveness, you can also use it to estimate how many sales are being made in a particular niche or genre before entering it.

Kindle Sales Rank	Daily Kindle Sales
1 - 100	3,000 - 500
100 - 500	500 - 200
500 - 1,000	200 - 150
1,000 - 2,000	150 - 75
2,000 - 3,000	75 - 50
3,000 - 4,000	50 - 40
4,000 - 5,000	40 - 30
5,000 - 7,500	30 - 15
7,500 - 10,000	15 - 10
10,000 - 12,500	10 - 8
12,500 - 15,000	8 - 7
15,000 - 20,000	6 - 5
20,000 - 25,000	5 - 4
25,000 - 30,000	4 - 3
30,000 - 40,000	3 - 2
40,000 - 50,000	2 - 1.5
50,000 - 70,000	1.5 - 1.0
70,000 - 100,000	1.0 - 0.5
> 100,000	< 0.5

Please note that these numbers are only approximate since Amazon does not publish sales figures based on the Kindle sales ranks of individual books. The figures in the table are based on sales of books by the author and the author's clients.

Selecting your categories in KDP

I mentioned earlier the unfortunate mismatch between the categories you assign to your book in KDP and the categories in Amazon's Kindle store. I also explained that you should choose your categories based on those in the Kindle store, since whenever your prospects search by category this is what they will see. All good so far... The problem comes when you actually have to select your book's categories within your KDP bookshelf.

The first thing to say is that you may be lucky and find that one or both of your chosen categories actually exist in KDP – the mismatch is not total!

If, however, you find a category that is "missing" then the first thing to do is put your book in whichever KDP category looks to be the closest match. Often you will find that when your book is published Amazon will "translate" this category into the one that you wanted anyway.

If your book ends up in one or more incorrect categories after publication don't worry – you can change your categories. The next step is to go back to your KDP bookshelf and try another close match to see if that will get your book into the right category.

If this still hasn't worked then it's time to contact the KDP support team. You do this by logging into your KDP account and then clicking the "Help" link near the top right of the page. Once on the help page (which is full of useful links, by the way) scroll down and at the bottom left you will find a "Contact Us" button. Click this and you will be able to submit a request to change your categories. It's a good idea to include a short explanation of why you think your book should be in the categories you are asking for. This does not guarantee you will get your categories changed, but the KDP support team are a pretty helpful bunch and will make the change for you if it makes sense to them.

Step 6: A great description

You will need to write a description for your book's Kindle page. A compelling description is an integral part of the sales process so this is worth spending some time on.

Remember that you need to take your prospective readers through a linear process before they will buy. First of all you catch their eye with a cover that "pops"; next you grab their attention with your title; then you hook them in further with your sub-title. Now it's time for your description to work its magic.

Craft a description that both excites your prospective customer, making them want to buy, and which also includes keywords that will increase the chances of people finding your book both on Amazon and through Google.

Your description is a chance to build in greater depth on what you've already achieved with your title and sub-title. If your book is fictional then this is your chance to introduce your protagonist and perhaps some other key characters as well as to say enough about the plot to leave people wanting to know "What happens next?"

Note that while keywords are important your description should still read naturally. If you stuff it full of keywords it will not only read badly it will appear contrived – something that will cost you sales. Besides, keyword stuffing may have worked fifteen years ago, but it doesn't work today!

You should use short paragraphs and bullet points (if appropriate) to break up the text in your description. Large, dense paragraphs of text are off putting and therefore less likely to get read. Shorter paragraphs are less imposing, plus they give people a faster sense of progress as they read, which encourages them to keep going.

Amazon allows you up to 4,000 characters in your book description. Use as many of those as you need to write a compelling description that gets your prospect to want to buy, but don't pad your description out for the sake of it. Doing so just reflects badly on you as a writer – hardly likely to encourage someone to buy.

In the next step we will be covering how to use Amazon HTML so that your description has maximum impact. For now just be aware that you will need to leave around 600 characters for the HTML code, meaning that you have around 3,400 characters to work with.

Step 7: Amazon HTML

I love Amazon HTML – it really enhances your description and you don't need to know a single line of code to use it (I'll explain why in a moment). Plus – inexplicably – relatively few authors take advantage of it so by using it your description will both stand out from the crowd and look much more professional.

Without Amazon HTML your description will appear as boring old plain text. With Amazon HTML you can use "Amazon orange" for the book title, bold text, italics, bullets and underlining to make key elements within your description stand out.

This works well for a couple of reasons. First of all it makes your description appear different and interesting. It is, therefore, more likely to get read, which will help increase your sales (as long as it's well written).

Second, it will increase engagement. We are "trained" to assume that text that is bolded, italicized, underlined or written as bullet points is important. By including these elements in your description you encourage people to keep reading through to find out what the next important element is.

Additionally, a lot of people will only skim through your description. Naturally, they will tend to skip straight to the emphasized text: this gives you a chance to draw their attention to the most important and compelling parts of your description.

You can do all of this without knowing a single line of Amazon HTML code. All you need to do is create a Word document that is formatted the way you want your description to appear on Amazon. Then you hire someone on Fiverr.com to create the code for you. This will cost you the princely sum of $5 and you will usually have the code back within a day.

Once you have your code simply go to your KDP bookshelf and copy and paste it into your book's description box (step 1 of the publishing process). Then save your changes and you're done.

Step 8: Social proof: customer reviews

Before you run the promotional campaigns for the launch of your book (which we'll be covering in the next chapter) you will need to get some positive customer reviews in place.

Having positive reviews for your book provides social proof that it is worth reading and so encourages people to buy it (or to download it if you are running a Kindle Free promo). If your book has no reviews in place then both downloads and sales will suffer as people will be reluctant to risk either their time or money on it.

I always aim to get at least five to ten good reviews in place before launching a book. It's true that the more reviews your book has the better, but there is a diminishing return and so once you have at least five in place I would say you're good to go.

One of the questions I'm often asked is "How can I get reviews in place before my book is published?" The short answer is that you can't. I need to make the distinction here between publishing your book and launching it so that the chronology makes sense.

By publishing I mean making your book "live" and available on Amazon. When I talk about launching your book I'm talking about running a promotion that will launch your book high up the bestseller list and get it established on Amazon.

So here's how to set up your customer reviews. First of all you publish your book – it's now live on Amazon. At this stage you don't do anything to promote it. What you can now start doing is preparing for your launch. It is during this stage that you get your initial five to ten customer reviews in place.

How do you get your initial reviews?

The first thing to mention is that, as you might expect, putting up fake reviews or paying for reviews is against Amazon's terms of service. Apart from being unethical it can lead to some or all of your reviews being taken down. It could even lead to your account being closed.

Amazon doesn't mind you asking for reviews, though you are not supposed to specify that they should be positive. You are also allowed to give out review copies of your book.

The way to get your initial reviews is simply to reach out to fans, followers and people in your market and ask them to leave an honest review. And while you can give out review copies I recommend you don't. Instead, set your book price temporarily at $0.99 (the lowest Amazon will allow) and ask people to buy a copy. This may sound a little bit cheeky, but most people won't mind – especially if you explain why:

The advantage of having people buy a copy is that when they post their review it shows up as a "Verified Purchase" review – this proves that the reviewer paid for the book. There is a growing awareness that reviews can be faked or bought and so this extra level of credibility will help your sales.

Amazon has removed a lot of reviews on the basis that they might be fake, though the algorithm responsible for this seems to have taken out a lot of legitimate reviews as well – call it collateral damage. Understandably, Amazon's priority is the experience of their customers and they don't want them exposed to fake reviews. Try not to do anything that will put your reviews or your account at risk.

Step 9: Social proof: editorial reviews

It's very common to see review quotes on the jacket of a physical book. Kindle books don't have a jacket, but what they do have is an "Editorial Reviews" section near the top of their Amazon page.

Like customer reviews, editorial reviews provide powerful social proof that your book is worth reading. Unlike customer reviews, however, you actually have control over your book's editorial reviews. This is great news because while editorial reviews look "official" and therefore credible, you can cherry pick only the most positive and convincing endorsements of your book.

Amazon stipulates that each editorial review should be limited to a one or two sentence quote and the source (whether a publication or individual) should be credited at the end of the quote.

For your Kindle book you are allowed up to 1,750 characters in your editorial reviews section. If you have a physical version of your book you are currently limited to 600 characters for that (though you still get the full 1,750 characters for the Kindle version).

Getting editorial reviews

Editorial reviews don't have to be from someone famous, though if they are that's certainly a bonus.

The best way to get editorial reviews is to network so that you are in a position to approach people in your field and ask for them. This is easier to do than ever now with email and social media. Most authors and experts will include contact details either in their book or on their website. Having said that, there is no substitute for meeting people at live events and building a relationship face to face whenever you get the chance.

People are busy so make it clear that you only need a one or two line quote and offer a review copy. To greatly increase your chances of getting a successful response include a pre-written quote that they can endorse (with or without edits), if they are happy with it, in order to save them time.

If you can get these organized in advance of your book launch that's great – it gives your book some instant credibility. However, if you can't then don't delay your launch. Just add them to Author Central as they come in.

Your Author Central account

Editorial reviews are added via your Author Central account.

Your Author Central account is distinct from both your KDP account and your Amazon account. It's designed to help authors promote their books and takes just a few moments to sign up for, which you can do using your Amazon account login details. You can set up your account by going to the Author Central homepage and clicking the "Join Now" button.

Once you have logged into your Author Central account click on the "Books" tab then select the book you want. Click on the "Editorial Reviews" tab and then click the "Edit" button in the "Review" section. This will open a pop-up window where you can add your editorial reviews.

Note that currently Author Central is only available on Amazon.com, Amazon.co.uk, Amazon.de, Amazon.fr and Amazon.co.jp (US, UK, Germany, France and Japan) and that it is necessary to set up a separate account for each site:

authorcentral.amazon.com
authorcentral.amazon.co.uk

authorcentral.amazon.de
authorcentral.amazon.fr
authorcentral.amazon.co.jp

Adding your editorial reviews is the last in the nine steps of this chapter's "building a bestseller" process. Once you complete these nine steps you will have in place extremely strong marketing foundations for your book and any future promotions will be much more successful as a result. Now it's time to move on and look at how to get Amazon to market your book for you and why it's so important.

Chapter 8:
Getting Amazon to market your book

STOP PRESS: Once you get your book to a certain tipping point Amazon will begin marketing it for you.

This is incredibly good news. In fact, I can't really overstate how important it is. Let me recap some of the reasons why this is such a big deal:

1. Amazon is the world's biggest <u>buyer</u> search engine
2. Amazon is the biggest bookshop in the world (600 million+ Kindle books sold in 2013)
3. Amazon is the world's most *trusted* online retailer
4. Amazon has 400,000,000+ credit cards on file: this allows "1-Click" impulse purchasing for Kindle books
5. Amazon will promote your books, putting them in front of *precisely targeted audiences* of <u>thousands of buyers</u>

The advertising that Amazon will give you for free is worth thousands of dollars. And as soon as Amazon starts promoting your book you can expect long-term organic sales. But there's a catch – there are a few things that you have to do before this will happen.

So how do you take advantage of Amazon's incredible promotional powers when launching your books?

Leveraging the 800 lb. Amazon Gorilla

When it comes to eBook sales (and book sales in general for that matter) Amazon is the 800 lb. Gorilla in the marketplace. It's hard to pin down exactly what percentage of eBook sales are through Amazon, but it's probably around 65% with the other "major" players in the eBook market only managing 35% between them.

This makes Amazon *the* place to be and if you can get Amazon to promote your book for you then suddenly you've got a pretty sweet deal! So how do you do it?

Well, once you've completed the nine steps to building a bestseller that we covered in the last chapter you will have already done much of what you need to do. As I explained, having these foundations in place will both increase the general sales of your book and make all your future marketing efforts more successful.

Nonetheless, the more successful your book is more Amazon will do to promote it. After all, Amazon is in the business of selling books and so it makes sense for it to promote books that have already begun to do well.

So, what we need to do as authors is prove to Amazon that our books are worth promoting. Running the perfect book launch is all about getting lots of sales in a short space of time and accelerating this process.

I mentioned earlier that Amazon update their bestseller lists every hour. For a launch to be successful it is, therefore, necessary to drive a lot of book sales in a short space of time. You don't have to worry about timing things down to the nearest hour, but what you should be aiming for is a spike in sales over a one to five day period (I'll cover how to time your promotions in the next chapter).

If you get your book launch right then you will get a sales "double whammy". Firstly, all the extra sales you drive from your promotion will push your book high up the bestseller lists. Secondly, as your book climbs the bestseller lists it will become highly visible on Amazon. This in turn leads to lots of organic sales that your book would not otherwise have got. These organic sales combined with sales from your promotion drive your book even higher.

And, because you have the "building a bestseller" foundations in place, your book will still be achieving good organic sales even when your launch is over. That's because your now high ranking book will be doing a great job of grabbing people's attention, hooking them in and making them want to buy.

This sets up the virtuous circle I talked about earlier, whereby high visibility leads to lots of organic sales, which maintains a high ranking and therefore continued visibility and so on.

Now that's not to say your book sales will not drop off over time – they will. But if you get these things right the drop off will be much slower and you will not need to continually promote your book to maintain worthwhile sales.

More Amazon benefits

The benefits of a successful launch aren't limited to high rankings in the bestseller charts. When your book sells lots of copies in a short space of time Amazon is quickly able to build up a picture of exactly where to promote it. Suddenly your book will start showing up all over the place on prime Amazon real estate – the "Also Bought" lists on the Amazon pages of other related books.

This is how Amazon gets your book in front of a laser targeted audience of buyers. Amazon knows that if a customer buys one book in a particular niche or genre then they are likely to buy several. That's why this strategy is so successful for them – and for you!

In fact, what Amazon will do to promote your books goes way beyond just the "Also Bought" lists. For example, if your book sells a lot of copies within a short time then it has a high chance of showing up in the "Hot New Releases" section within its category listings. And if it has a high average review rating it may also show up in the "Top Rated" section of its category listings as well.

It's a great feeling to see your book at the top of the bestseller list and showing up as a "Hot New Release" and a "Top Rated" book all at the same time:

Here is a list of places where Amazon may promote your book on its category listing pages:

Hot New Releases

Best Sellers [year to date]

Movers & Shakers

Most Wished For

Gift Ideas

And we're only just getting started here. On the pages of related books Amazon will promote your books in all these different areas:

Customers Who Bought This Item Also Bought

What Other Items Do Customers Buy After Viewing This Item?

Customers Who Highlighted This Item Also Highlighted

Look for Similar Items by Category

Your Recently Viewed Items and Featured Recommendations

Customers Who Bought Items in Your Recent History Also Bought

That's a lot of places for your book to show up!

In addition to these and all of the bestseller lists your book will appear on, Amazon continually makes recommendations to people based on their purchasing history – in other words, the more successful your book is the more likely Amazon is to recommend it to the people who are most likely to buy it. Laser targeting!

Bestseller benefits

If your book becomes a category #1 bestseller and then Amazon will highlight it in the "Also Bought" lists with a #1 bestseller tag like this:

Moneyball (Movie Tie-in Edition) (Movie …
› Michael Lewis
★★★★½ (950)
#1 Best Seller
in Baseball Statistics
Kindle Edition
$9.97

This really helps your book to stand out and is also great social proof – more incentive, if any were needed, to get your book to #1 bestseller in one or more of its categories.

Being the author of a bestselling book is also incredible positioning. It is something that you can add to the cover of your book that will increase sales. And once you have one bestseller you can put "By bestselling author..." or words to that effect on your other books as well.

If you sell any kind of product or service that relates to your book then being a bestselling author will give you tremendous credibility – instantly positioning you as an expert authority and settings you apart from and above the rest of your marketplace. Your bestselling book can be leveraged to create free media coverage, to win more clients and to increase your prices.

Taking screenshots

Once you become a bestselling author you have that status for ever. It's a great feeling and it's also great to be able to share your success with people. For this reason, I strongly recommend that you monitor your launch promotion closely and get screenshots of your book's success. Apart from the fact that it's great to watch your book climb up the Kindle rankings and hit the bestseller lists (especially when it gets to #1) the screenshots you take will provide future proof of your book's success and can be used in any presentations and marketing materials you create.

Check out this screenshot for Flash Boys – the latest book by Michael Lewis:

It totally dominates the page, showing a total of seven times either as the Kindle edition or as the hardcover edition! Notice also how the cover really pops off the page immediately drawing in the eye – particularly in comparison to the other books there.

By the way, in case you hadn't guessed, I'm a big fan of Michael Lewis and I'll be picking up this book in a couple of weeks to read when I go on holiday!

Tracking your book

Apart from taking screenshots there are a number of other ways in which you can track the sales and success of your book. Here are the places that I use to track both my own books and those of my clients:

1. KDP Reports

The Reports section of your KDP account has some great tracking tools; especially now that Amazon has introduced its new Sales Dashboard.

Here's a screenshot of the Sales Dashboard for a client's book that I recently ran a promotion for. It's pretty clear from this picture what kind of impact that the right promotion can have:

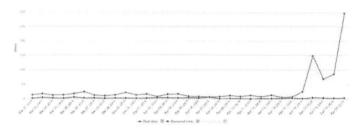

2. Author Central

Your Author Central account allows you to track your books' Kindle rankings over time. This can be very helpful if you ever want to look back at your book sales to see how well a particular promotion worked.

If you have physical versions of your books – for example, CreateSpace versions – you can also track those sales here as well, since Amazon has teamed up with Nielsen BookScan

The other thing you can track in Author Central is your Amazon author rank. Your author rank is based on the aggregate sales of all your books and shows you where you rank among all Amazon authors both now and over time.

3. eBookTracker

This is a free service provided by the Kindle Nation Daily website. It allows you to track not just your own books, but books by other authors as well. One of the things I like about eBookTracker is that it shows you both the highest and lowest rankings for the books you are tracking and will give you an hourly breakdown for the most recent 24 hours.

Here's the link for your free eBookTracker account:

tracker.kindlenationdaily.com

OK, so I hope I've convinced you how important it is to get your book to that magic tipping point where Amazon starts promoting it for you. This process is inextricably linked to running a successful launch promotion – something which has the huge built-in benefit of getting your book to rank high in the Kindle bestseller lists. Not only does it make you a bestselling author, it also gives you tremendous credibility and positions you as an expert in your field.

Your successful book launch is also what gives Amazon the proof that it's worth promoting and the sales data it needs to put your book in front of a laser targeted audience of Kindle book buyers. This in turn leads to long-term success and organic sales for your book.

So the next question is: how do you run a successful Kindle launch promotion? That's what we're going to cover in the next chapter.

Chapter 9:
The perfect launch

In this chapter we're going to look at how to set up and run the perfect launch for your book – one that will rocket it up the bestseller lists and set it up for long-term success.

The chapter is organized as follows:

Part I: The launch sequence

Part II: Kindle Free promo vs. Kindle Countdown

Part III: The Kindle Free plus $0.99 "hybrid" alternative

Part IV: Timing your launch

Part V: Kindle Free promos

Part VI: $0.99 promotions

Part VII: Kindle Countdown

Part I looks at the sequence of publishing and then launching your book. Part II will look at the pros and cons of Kindle Free promos vs. Kindle Countdowns. Then, in Part III, we'll look at a "hybrid" alternative that allows you to get the best of both worlds. Part IV covers the timing of your launch – what day should it start and how long should it run for? In Parts V and VI, respectively, we'll look at how to set up and run the two elements of the "hybrid" alternative: the Kindle Free promo and the $0.99 promotion. Finally, Part VII will cover how to set up and run a Kindle Countdown promotion.

Part I: The launch sequence

Let's start by looking at the launch sequence in proper "countdown" order:

5. Choose your launch date
4. Publish your book
3. Get pre-launch reviews in place
2. Get advertising set up in advance
1. Launch!

The good news is that by the time you come to launch your book you will have already done a lot of the hard work: Publishing your book was the subject of chapter 6 and we looked out how to get pre-launch reviews (both customer and editorial) in chapter 7. So that just leaves choosing your launch date, setting up your advertising and hitting the launch button!

In this section we're just going to cover choosing your launch date and how that relates to the timing of getting your reviews in place and your advertising set up. The process of actually setting up that advertising as well as what sort of promotions you should run will be covered in the remainder of the chapter.

Choosing your launch date

There are two main things you need to consider when picking the launch date for your book. The first is how long it will take you to get your pre-launch reviews in place. The second is how much lead-in time you need to allow to get your advertising set up.

We'll be covering advertising in detail in step 2 of the launch sequence, but I just want to mention a couple of things about it here. The first is that you shouldn't be afraid of spending money on advertising. The fact is, your advertising campaigns should perform well enough to be "self-liquidating" or better. Self-liquidating means that the revenue you bring in from the campaign will cover your advertising costs. In reality you are likely to actually make a profit.

The second thing I wanted to mention about advertising at this point concerns choosing your launch date. How long should you leave between publishing your book and starting your launch?

The exact amount of time will vary depending on how big you plan your launch to be, but I would budget for a minimum of a week. In my experience these things usually take longer than you expect!

First of all, you need time to get your reviews in place. Naturally, there will be people who agree to write a review with the best of intentions and either forget or don't get it done until way after your planned launch date. What I would suggest here is that if you want five reviews then ask at least ten people. If they all "show up" great, but if only half do then you've still hit your numbers. It's also important to make people aware that you have a fixed launch date and need the reviews in place by then.

Secondly, the task of booking your advertising in is not quite as straightforward as it first appears. There are lots of websites where you can advertise free and discounted Kindle books. Many of them, however, require books to have a minimum number of reviews as well as a minimum average rating – typically four stars or more. So, for these sites you can't even book your advertising until your reviews are in place.

Plus, it's not simply a case of "turning up on the day" and booking your ads. On most sites (at least the ones that are worth using) you will need to book your ad at least two or three days in advance. The more popular sites now require anything from one to three weeks' notice, and the most popular can be booked out more than two months in advance.

I wouldn't suggest you wait that long to run your launch – you can always use the most popular sites to boost your sales post-launch. However, allowing a couple of weeks between publication and launch will give you the time you need to get on most of the important sites. I'll give you lists of both free and discount sites later on in this chapter.

Getting your advertising set up and setting up your promotion so that it will launch automatically we will cover later in this chapter.

Part II: Kindle Free promo vs. Kindle Countdown

At the start of chapter 6 we looked at the two different types of promotions that Amazon offers you if your book is enrolled in KDP Select. These are the Kindle Free promo and the Kindle Countdown.

If for any reason your book is not enrolled in KDP Select you may want to skip ahead to Parts III and VI, which cover the $0.99 promotion alternative to the KDP Select based options. That said, you may find this to be useful background information for future reference.

In this section we'll look at the pros and cons of your two KDP Select based options: the Kindle Free promo vs. the Kindle Countdown.

How does the launch actually work?

The idea behind your book launch is simple: to sell as many copies as possible in a short space of time so that you can rocket your book up the Kindle bestseller lists. And the best way to sell lots of books in a short space of time is to offer people a special time limited promotional deal. That's where the KDP Select promotions come into play, but which one should you use? Remember, you can choose one or the other in each 90 day enrolment period, but not both.

The Kindle Free promo

There are, of course, pros and cons to both types of promotion. Let's start by looking at Kindle Free promos.

You don't get paid!

The most obvious downside to running a Kindle Free promotion is that you don't get paid! It may seem very counterintuitive to give thousands of copies of your book away for free after working so hard on it. The reality, though, is that it can be more than worth it to get your book established on Amazon. It is true that a Kindle Free promo will cut into your pool of potential book buyers, but the effect is fairly marginal – we are talking about a small fraction of potential buyers here.

Thousands of downloads

The biggest advantage of running a Kindle Free promo is that you will get many more downloads if your book is free then you will get sales at a discount – even at the $0.99 minimum Kindle book price.

This is significant because the more downloads your book gets the more data Amazon has to work with. A Kindle Free promo can easily generate several thousand downloads. Amazon is able to analyze the purchasing history of everyone downloading your book and quickly build a picture of where to promote it. This is what gives your book momentum when the free promotion ends and your book switches back to paid.

Now, not all of these downloads will be well targeted. That's because when your book is free it will be downloaded by many people who would not otherwise have bought it. As a result, you're likely to find all sorts of unrelated books (that have done well in the free Kindle book charts at the same time) showing up in your book's "Also Bought" list. As your book climbs the category bestseller lists, however, the downloads will become increasingly targeted. It is these downloads that will give your book most of its momentum when it switches from free to paid, since it is when your book shows up on the pages of other related books that organic sales are generated.

Until the spring of 2012 a book's free downloads actually counted towards its paid Kindle rank at the end of the free promotion. This meant that the momentum from a Kindle Free promo could carry a book high into the paid charts even without these organic sales. However, in March 2012 Amazon introduced an algorithm change that reduced the weighting of a free download to around 10% that of a paid download. Then in May 2012 another algorithm change eliminated the influence of free downloads entirely.

At the time, many in the Kindle self-publishing space saw this as a terrible development. To read some of the things posted on blogs and in forums you would have thought that this marked the end for self-published Kindle authors! Clearly this has not been the case as Kindle self-publishing continues to go from strength to strength.

My personal view is that Amazon's algorithm changes in the spring of 2012 were a good thing since for books to succeed now they need to be able to stand up in their own right as purchased books. It's no longer simply possible to piggy-back off thousands of free downloads.

The reason for this Amazon algorithm history lesson, by the way, is that a lot of the advice on the subject published online prior to May 2012 (and which may have been good advice at the time) is now out of date. If you make the mistake of following it you are likely to get disappointing results.

Ranking high in the free Kindle "bestseller" lists

One key benefit of running a Kindle Free promo is that your book has the chance to rank highly in the free Kindle "bestseller" lists.

I've put "bestseller" in quotes because, in my opinion, this does not actually make your book a bestseller – even though that is the terminology that Amazon uses to describe the lists. I say this because when people think about a bestselling book they naturally assume that it's a bestseller because a large number of people have paid for it – the clue is in the name! I simply don't believe that a book that ranks highly in the free Kindle charts is a bestseller in the true and honest sense of the word.

That's not to say, however, that there are no benefits to your book becoming a free "bestseller". One client of mine published a Kindle book that hit #1 in the "Health Care Delivery" category during its free promotion. A few days later he was giving a presentation to a group of doctors in San Diego during which he showed them a screenshot of his book at number one. Despite the fact that it was number one in the free "bestseller" list and that this was clear from the screenshot he told me that it had a profound effect on the doctors. Immediately they became more receptive to what he had to say, treated him as more of an expert and became much more interested in doing business with him – all because he was the author of a #1 "bestselling" book in the free Kindle charts.

Building your list and selling backend products or services

By getting your book into the hands of thousands of people a Kindle Free promo can be helpful in building your list or helping you sell backend products or services.

To complicate matters, however, the level of engagement you get when you give your book away for free is far less than when people have to pay for it – even if they are only paying a nominal amount such as $0.99.

The fact is that many of the people who download your book for free will never bother to read it. There is a tendency to for people to grab Kindle books when they are free "just in case" – after all, free is hard to resist and there's no cost to them if they never get round to it. Quite simply, people put much less value on things they don't have to pay for. This means that as a list building tool a Kindle Free promo is not as effective as you might imagine.

This is not the only thing to consider. Those readers who have paid something for your book are more likely to purchase your other books and/or backend products or services than those who got it for free. In other words, an opt-in list of people who got your book for free is not the equal of an opt-in list of book buyers.

Of course, the numbers will be different for every book. The more powerful your Call to Action, the more compelling your offer, the more times you can weave your CTAs into your book the more opt-ins you will get. It may be that the benefits of getting your book into the hands of many more people for free outweigh the disadvantages of lower engagement levels.

Unfortunately, the only way to know for sure is to test. If you only plan to promote your book once – i.e., at the time of launch – then there's really no need to worry about testing. However, if your book is part of a long-term marketing strategy designed to position you and generate back end sales of your product or service then testing is something you should seriously consider.

(If you don't ever plan to test your promotions then skip ahead until you get to the **Kindle Countdowns** sub-heading.)

How to test

If you decide to test then you will need to run two separate promotions each of which will test three separate variables. Only then will you know whether it makes financial sense (when running a promotion) to offer your book for free or to discount it to $0.99.

You will of course need to run one Kindle Free promo and one Kindle Countdown, meaning that your tests will need to take place over two consecutive 90 day KDP Select enrolment periods. If you wish to speed things up you could run the $0.99 promo that we'll be covering in Parts III and VI as an alternative to the Kindle Countdown promo – just to be aware that a $0.99 promo will not be as effective as a Kindle Countdown promo, so your results will be less accurate.

The three variables that you will be testing for are:

1. The total number of sales or downloads during the promotion
2. The number (and percentage) of opt-ins that result
3. The number (and percentage) of opt-ins who convert to buying customers when presented with an identical offer

The reports available within your KDP account will give you all the information you need to track than total number of sales or downloads during each promotion period.

In order to track the number of opt-ins that result from each promotion you will need to set up a distinct squeeze page and a separate email list within your auto responder for each promotion.

The squeeze pages you set up will, of course, have different addresses and so just before the start of each promotion you will have to upload a slightly revised version of your book. The only change that you will make is to the opt-in links that accompany your Calls to Action. This way the readers who download or buy your book during that promotion will be directed to the specific squeeze page that you set up and, if they opt-in, added to the corresponding email list.

As soon as the promotion ends you must re-upload the normal version of your book – the one that links to your normal squeeze page. There will be a few people who buy your book and opt-in after the promotion has ended, but before the normal version is back on sale. Don't worry – this is unavoidable and should only have a marginal impact on your test results.

The final step in testing is to run an offer to the email list you have built from the promotion. This offer must be identical in every way for both promotions – the same offer, the same price, the same emails, the same videos, etc. Even though you cannot run your two promotions simultaneously, you should aim to start and finish them on the same days of the week and to run your offers the same number of days after your promotions. The longer you wait to run the offer the colder your leads will be and so you don't want this to be a factor.

Having done all this you will have the information you need to be able to calculate whether a free or a $0.99 promotion makes the most sense for you financially. The calculation you need to make is as follows:

Total number of sales or downloads x percentage of opt-ins x percentage converting to buying customers

Let's look at two hypothetical promotions by way of comparison:

Kindle Free promo:

10,000 downloads x 10% opt-in rate x 5% conversion = **50 sales**

Kindle Countdown:

3,000 sales x 25% opt-in rate x 10% conversion = **75 sales**

In our hypothetical example, the Kindle Countdown wins by a wide margin – leading to an additional 25 sales. That would be equal to 50% more business generated and demonstrates why testing is so important.

In reality, it should not actually be necessary to do these calculations since you will simply be able to look at the number of sales generated by each promotion, though it's nice to have the data to be able to see how you arrived at those sales.

You could summarize the impact of a Kindle Free promo as being broader and the impact of a Kindle Countdown promo as being deeper. Which of these will be best for your business, however, will only be revealed if you test both alternatives.

Kindle Countdowns

We've already covered a lot of what you need to know about Kindle Countdowns over the last few pages (and at the start of chapter 6) so this section will be a fairly brief summary.

Let's start with the pros of Kindle Countdowns. First of all, unlike the Kindle Free promo, you get paid! Not only do you get paid, you can discount your book to below $2.99 and still get paid 70% royalties, rather than 35% – the only proviso being that it must have been in the 70% bracket immediately prior to the promo.

Another big benefit is that every single sale counts towards your paid Kindle sales rank. Each sale you make pushes your book higher up the bestseller lists and increases its visibility and in turn the number of organic sales.

The sales you make when running a Kindle Countdown are much more highly targeted than the downloads you get when running a Kindle Free promo. This means more reader engagement, a higher percentage of opt-ins and a higher likelihood of someone leaving a review.

The key downside of a Kindle Countdown compared to a Kindle Free promo is that the number of sales you make will be far less than the number of downloads you could expect. Whether or not the benefits of increased engagement (Kindle Countdown) are outweighed by the greater number of downloads (Kindle Free promo) can only be determined, as we have seen, by testing.

There is one other big drawback to running a Kindle Countdown when you are launching your book. And this is that before your Kindle Countdown can start your book must have been enrolled in KDP Select for at least 30 days and the price cannot have changed for at least 30 days. This means that if you planned to launch your book using a Kindle Countdown you would have to wait a month after publishing before you could start. While you will almost certainly need to wait at least a week or two to get your reviews and advertising in place, a month is a long time to wait with few if any sales.

Getting the best of both worlds?

I mentioned at the beginning of the chapter a "hybrid" alternative to the either/or choice of running a Kindle Free promo or a Kindle Countdown. Now that we've got a clear understanding of the pros and cons of both options let's have a look at this alternative.

Part III: The Kindle Free plus $0.99 "hybrid" alternative

When launching your book it's vital that you get as many sales as possible in a short space of time to take advantage of the way that Amazon calculates its bestseller lists. Those lists are updated hourly and there is a very strong recency bias in the way that they are calculated. In other words, you ideally want to concentrate your promotional efforts, and therefore sales, into no more than one or two days or as close to that as the available advertising slots will allow.

The hybrid alternative to simply running one of the standard KDP Select promos involves starting your launch with a Kindle Free promo. Then, immediately upon that finishing, you run a $0.99 promotion until your book peaks in the bestseller lists.

186

A $0.99 promotion is something that you can run any time and which is independent of KDP Select. If for any reason your book is not enrolled in KDP Select then this is the type of promo you should run when you launch your book.

Here's why this double back-to-back promo works so well and why it really is the closest you'll get to the best of both worlds. First of all, you run a Kindle Free promo (I'll explain exactly how in Part V) and your book gets all the benefits associated with that as described above. You should run this Kindle Free promo for the full five days available – we'll look at why in the next section.

At the start of day six your $0.99 promotion kicks in. At this point your book will already have significant momentum from the organic sales generated by the Kindle Free promo. When you immediately follow it with the $0.99 promotion it will be like adding rocket fuel to the fire.

By pricing your Kindle book at $0.99 you turn it into the ultimate impulse purchase. That, combined with Amazon's ingenious "1-Click" purchasing, will generate a flood of sales that will rocket your book up the *paid* bestseller lists for its categories and sub-categories. I'll explain exactly how to set up and run your $0.99 promotion in Part VI.

There is no set time for which you should run the $0.99 promotion. That's because you should keep it going until your book's Kindle sales rank has peaked. This is likely to be within the first two or three days, but will depend very much on the amount of advertising you have got going out, when it starts (ideally on day six) and how many organic sales your book generates as it rises through the bestseller lists.

The only way to know when your book has peaked is to track it closely – something you should be doing anyway so that you can get your screenshots. We've already covered the most important tracking tools that you have available to you.

Once you see that your book's sales are dropping off you have a choice. You can either leave it at $0.99 – at least for a time – to take advantage of the increased sales that this price generates. Or you can switch back to the book's long-term sales price, which – assuming it is $2.99 or more – is likely to generate you significantly more royalties.

Part IV: Timing your launch

The day you choose to start your book launch matters – in fact, it matters a lot!

Have a look at the Google trends analysis below. It shows search volume for the term "free kindle books" over a 90 day period. The pattern it shows is remarkably consistent with the peak volume for every single week coming on a Sunday! Saturday, by the way, is usually a close second and occasionally (though not in this chart) it overtakes Sunday.

Every single red arrow on this three-month chart is pointing to a Sunday! So how do you take advantage of this knowledge to get the best results?

Well, I've already mentioned that Amazon uses a moving average with a strong recency bias to calculate its bestseller lists. I've also discussed how if you're running a Kindle Free promo you should use all five days at once for maximum momentum. And now we know that the two days of the week when you can expect the most downloads are Saturday and Sunday.

To get the best possible results when you run your Kindle Free promo you need to take advantage of the extra weekend demand for free Kindle books. Your goal should be to have the number of downloads of your book peak on a Sunday and this can only happen if the promotion has enough momentum going into the Sunday.

That's why I always start my Kindle Free promos on a Thursday. By the time you get to Sunday it already has three days' momentum, which includes Saturday – the second best day of the week.

This means is that Sunday will be day four of your Kindle Free promo and Monday day five, with your $0.99 promotion starting on the Tuesday.

You could start your Kindle Free promo a day earlier so that it finishes on the Sunday, but I like to run it through to Monday because with fewer overall downloads on a Monday it is less competitive and therefore easier to rank highly on the back of all the momentum your promo has already generated.

During your Kindle Free promo it's a good idea to have your book priced at its normal full price within your KDP bookshelf. Amazon will automatically switch it to free for the duration of the promotion regardless of the price it's set at in KDP. However, next to the "free" price they will also display the normal list price struck through with a line. You want people to see the full list price so they can see how much they are saving.

For this reason I recommend that you don't change the list price to $0.99 until a few hours before the promotion is about to end (I allow 12 hours for the change to go through). Then, at the end of the Kindle Free promo your book's price will automatically switch to $0.99.

The length of your $0.99 promotion will depend on when your book peaks in the paid charts as discussed in Part III above.

Be aware – for example, if sending out promotional emails – when setting up your Kindle Free promos that Amazon will start and finish them at approximately midnight Pacific Standard Time on your selected days. (This is not the case for Kindle Countdown promos where you are able to choose the precise hour that you would like them to start and finish.)

"system latencies"

If your book is ranking highly in the Kindle free "bestseller" lists on the final day of your Kindle Free promo you may want to end it slightly early. That's because due to what Amazon described as "system latencies" it can sometimes take a few hours for your book to stop showing in the free listings even after it reverts to paid. The advantage of this is that lots of people click on free book listings and, despite discovering that is no longer free, some of them will be interested enough to buy it anyway – especially if it is priced at only $0.99. This can give the paid part of your launch campaign a nice boost.

If there's no delay then "no harm, no foul" – all that happens is that you don't get the boost; on the other hand, if there is a delay you will benefit from an extra boost in sales immediately prior to the start of your $0.99 promotion.

The most wonderful time of the year!

There's a particular time of year that's awesome for Kindle book launches. If you happen to be bringing a book out around this time then you should definitely consider taking advantage of it.

In fact, it's a specific eight day period – starting with Christmas Day and finishing on New Year's Day. This is when not only do lots of people get brand new Kindles and iPads as presents, they also have the time to download and consume both free and paid Kindle books.

Look at the Google trends chart below showing "free kindle books" searches all the way back to November 2007 when Kindle was first launched. Every single one of the five major peaks is for the month of December and if you were to drill down into the individual months you would see it was for the Christmas week.

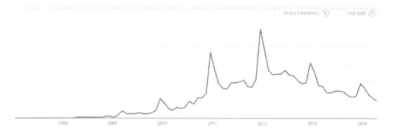

By the way, don't be alarmed at the drop off in the number of searches in the last couple of years. Kindle book sales are still trending strongly upwards (as we saw at the start of the book). What's happening is that, for the most part, the millions of existing Kindle owners already know how to find free Kindle books if they want them so they no longer need to search. Search volume will also spike higher if a hotly anticipated new Kindle or iPad comes on the market in time for Christmas.

Part V: Kindle Free promos

When it comes to running your Free Kindle promo there are two steps that we need to cover. The first is how you set the promotion up in your KDP account. The second is how you promote the promotion: how to get the word out to maximize the number of downloads you get.

Step 1: Setting up your Kindle Free promo

Setting up your Kindle Free promo could hardly be easier. Simply go to your KDP Bookshelf and click on the "Manage Benefits" link next to the book you want to promote (note that you will only see this link for books that are enrolled in KDP Select).

On the next page you will see a button that allows you to choose either a Kindle Countdown Deal or a Free Book Promotion. Select Free Book Promotion and click the button. Then click the link next to it that says "Create a new Free Book Promotion Deal for this book".

This will take you on to a new page where you can set the start and end dates for your Kindle Free promo. Once you've done this click the "Save Changes" button and your Kindle Free promo is all set up!

Pricing

A quick reminder that if you're going to run a $0.99 promotion immediately after your Kindle Free promo then you should set the price of your book at $0.99 around 12 hours *before* your Kindle Free promo ends.

All five days at once

I've already said you'll get the best results if you use all five of your Kindle Free promo days together. At this point I need to share another quick history lesson with you – again, this is so you don't end up following advice that will steer you wrong because it is out of date.

Remember those algorithm changes I mentioned earlier? Well, prior to their introduction an effective tactic was to split up your five Kindle Free promo days into two separate two or three day promotions. Because the free downloads had some weighting towards your paid Kindle sales rank it was easy to get a big boost up the paid charts each time you ran one of these mini promotions. Since May 2012 this is no longer the case.

There are two main benefits of running Kindle Free promos today, both of which we've already looked at. The first is to get your book established on Amazon; the second is to get your book into the hands of thousands of people to help build your list and/or to generate sales of your other books, products or services.

The first of these – getting your book established – only requires you to run a Kindle Free promo once (for the full five days). After that Amazon will have the information it needs to start promoting your book effectively. Therefore, the benefits of running a second Kindle Free promo are negligible as far as getting your book promoted by Amazon is concerned.

This leaves getting your book into the hands of thousands of people, and this is a reason why you might want to run more than one Kindle Free promo. Of course, the only way to know for sure is to test.

Step 2: Promoting your Kindle Free promo

Amazon will help you promote your free book, but if you make the effort to "prime the pump" your Kindle Free promo will be much more successful – potentially giving you thousands of extra downloads. The way you prime the pump is to advertise your free promotion. This gets your book climbing up the charts early in your promo, increasing its visibility so that organic downloads follow.

The key to successfully advertising your promotion is to apply the 80/20 Principle. There are many things that you could do to promote your books, but the reality is that a small handful of them will generate the vast majority of your results. Here are the ones that we are going to use:

1. Free Kindle book sites
2. Fiverr promotional gigs

3.   Facebook groups
4.   Facebook promoted posts
5.   Twitter
6.   Email lists (other people's)

How much should you spend?

I recommend that only about a third of your advertising budget is spent on your Kindle Free promo and that you spend the rest on your $0.99 promotion, with the lion's share being spent advertising on websites that promote either free or discount Kindle books.

In total I have spent as little as $200 and as much as $1,000 or more on a book launch. You can get some pretty good results for $200 – but, of course, the more you spend the better your results are likely to be.

1. Free Kindle book sites

The most important weapons in our advertising arsenal are websites that promote free Kindle books. Many of these are high traffic sites with lots of social media followers and large email lists. Advertising on these sites is very cost effective and will allow you to reach thousands of potential readers, all of whom are interested in free Kindle books, at very low cost.

I set my advertising up so that some of it begins on day one of the Kindle Free promo (Thursday) to get the promotion off to a good start and help build momentum. I then have the bulk of my advertising going out on the Saturday and Sunday when I can expect the peak number of downloads.

Booking your advertising

I explained earlier that you need to allow some lead-in time for setting up your advertising. Usually, less notice is required to book advertising if you are promoting your book for free as opposed to promoting it when it is discounted. Nonetheless, you will need to set your advertising up a few days in advance and, for a lot of sites, have a minimum number of reviews in place – typically, with at least a four star average.

Sites that promote free Kindle books

If I'm paying to promote my book I want it to be on a site that gets a worthwhile amount of traffic. As a rule of thumb, I look for sites that have a worldwide Alexa.com rank of 250,000 or less and/or a US Alexa.com rank of 100,000 or less (because the vast majority of my Kindle book sales are in the US). If you're not familiar with Alexa.com it ranks the world's websites. You can use it for free to check the ranking of any site – the lower the ranking the better, with the world's most popular website at any given time having an Alexa rank of 1.

Here is a non-exhaustive list of sites where you can promote free Kindle books and which either fit those criteria (at the time of writing) or which are free or cheap enough to still be worth advertising on:

AskDavid.com

AwesomeGang.com

BargaineBookHunter.com

BookBub.com

BookGoodies.com

DailyFreeBooks.com

DigitalBookToday.com

eBooksHabit.com

eReaderGirl.com

eReaderLove.com

eReaderNewsToday.com

fkBooksandTips.com

FreeBookDude.com

FreeDigitalReads.com

IndieBookofTheDay.com

KindleBookPromos.Luckycinda.com

KindleNationDaily.com
PixelofInk.com
PixelScroll.com
TheeReaderCafe.com
TheKindleBookReview.net
VesselProject.com
WorldLiteraryCafe.com

Note that where words have been capitalized it is to make the URLs easier to read in case you need to type them – they are not case sensitive.

Please don't feel that you have to use all of these sites! A handful of high-ranking sites should deliver you good results. Once your book starts to gain traction and rise through the free "bestseller" lists Amazon will start doing a lot of the heavy lifting for you.

Bear in mind also that, as a general rule, those sites that promote both free and discount Kindle books will not advertise your book when it is discounted if they have just advertised it for free. Therefore, if you are planning on a large budget, make sure you still have enough good discount Kindle book sites to advertise on after you've set up your Kindle Free promo advertising.

2. Fiverr promotional gigs

There are so many things you can get done on Fiverr.com. Something I've had great success with is buying Fiverr gigs from people offering to promote free and/or discount Kindle books on Facebook or Twitter or to email lists or via blogs.

To be honest, I was very skeptical about whether or not these types of gigs would generate any worthwhile results. Fortunately, I gave them a try using bitly.com shortened URLs to track the results. After receiving several hundred click throughs in the first campaign I've continue to use them ever since.

I would recommend spending around 10% to 20% of your budget on Fiverr gigs, which should be split between your Kindle Free promo and your $0.99 promotion. Make sure, when purchasing your gigs, that you specify which days you want them to go out.

3. Facebook groups

There are hundreds of Kindle author groups on Facebook and many of these will allow you to promote your free or discounted books. When posting on Facebook it's possible to link directly to your book's Amazon page and, usually, Facebook will display an image of your book, which helps draw attention.

It makes sense that the more active you are within a group the more of a response you are likely to get when posting. However, you may want to limit yourself to being active in only a small number of groups as this is not likely to be an efficient use of your time in terms of return on investment.

Posting about your offer in Facebook groups is not something that is likely to generate vast numbers of downloads of your book. It is, however, free and easy to do and does not take a lot of time – therefore it's worth adding to your list of promotional activities.

4. Facebook promoted posts

Something that is likely to get more significant results is running Facebook promoted posts either on your own relevant page, if you have one, or on other people's.

A Facebook promoted post is what is known as "native advertising". What this means is that, unlike and the ads that appear on the right side of the page, it appears in a person's newsfeed in the same way as content from their friends would. By appearing more like regular content native ads get much higher click through rates and can be much more cost effective than traditional Facebook ads.

Facebook promoted posts can either be shown to people who like that page and their friends or it can be targeted at specific groups of Facebook users based on their demographics and interests. Both are effective ways of advertising, though you may need to consider the potential reach of the two options, particularly if you are planning a large ad spend. This is easy to do as it's something Facebook shows you as you set the promotion up.

Promoting posts on other people's pages

How do you run a promoted post on a page you don't own? By searching for pages whose audiences are likely to appreciate your type of book and reaching out to the page owners. It's often possible to message page admins directly through Facebook, though not all pages allow this. If you can't message directly you may be able to contact the page owner via their website. Either way, reach out to them and ask if you could pay to promote a post on their page. You will, of course, have to pay both the cost of the promotion (whatever you're prepared to spend) and a fee to them for promoting via their page.

There's no set fee for running a promoted post, though it is likely to run to anywhere from $10 to $50 depending on the popularity and reach of the page. Most page owners will not be used to being asked to promote a post so you will need to either ask how much it would cost or make an offer – and perhaps negotiate. Just be sure not to spend too much on the fee otherwise your advertising will cease to be cost effective.

If your book both aligns with the page and is being offered for free then it has two advantages from the point of view of the page owner. First, it falls into the category of good content. Second, by offering good content for free they will be able to generate goodwill on the part of their audience. In situations where this is the case not only are you more likely to get a "yes" you will probably end up paying a smaller fee.

5. Twitter

Similar to Facebook, Twitter can be a cost effective way of reaching a large number of targeted prospects. As well as tweeting out to your own followers, if you have them, you can adopt a similar strategy to the Facebook promoted posts strategy above.

Search Twitter for people with large numbers of followers who are likely to be interested in your book and reach out to them asking if they will tweet to promote your offer. As with Facebook promoted posts, there is no set fee so ask or make an offer based on the number of followers the person has and how engaged they appear to be. Try also to negotiate multiple tweets over the promotion period to maximize their reach.

I prefer to craft my own tweets rather than relying on people to do them. When crafting tweets don't forget to make use of both shortened URLs (bitly.com allows you to track how many click throughs you get) and any relevant hashtags that will help people in the Twittersphere discover your tweet.

6. Email lists (other people's)

The reason I've added "other people's" in brackets is because if you have an email list of your own I want you to hold it in reserve for when you start your $0.99 promotion. That's because, of all the lists you email, your own list is likely to be the most responsive. It makes sense, therefore, to ask for their help when it matters most – i.e., when you want to get your book rocketing up the *paid* bestseller lists.

If you can get people to email their lists at the start of your $0.99 promotion, rather than when your book is free, then do so. The reason I am bringing up other people's email lists here is that getting people to promote your book when it is free is an easier sell.

The "usual rules" apply when trying to leverage other people's lists: Just as with Facebook and Twitter reach out to people with audiences who are likely to be interested in your book. Again, if what you're asking them to promote is both good quality content and free you are more likely to get a "yes".

Broadly speaking the cost will depend on the size of the list and can be anywhere from a few dollars to several hundred dollars. However, before agreeing on a fee try to gauge how responsive the list is. A highly responsive list of 10,000 may be better than an unresponsive list of 100,000. If the list owner is unwilling to give you any information about the responsiveness of their list then consider looking elsewhere.

Follow up

Is there anything you can be doing to encourage people to post updates after they've made their initial posts, or sent their tweets or emails? How about updating them to say that your book has hit a certain milestone, such as bestseller in a certain category (or, better still, #1 bestseller) or that it's been downloaded a thousand times, for example? You could also try to get them to send a reminder when there's only one day left for people to get your book for free.

Part VI: $0.99 promotions

As I said earlier, running a $0.99 promotion immediately after a Kindle Free promo is the book launch equivalent of adding rocket fuel to a fire. It's where we bring everything we've done so far together to launch your book to the top of the paid bestseller lists.

All the "building a bestseller" foundations that you worked so hard to create and all the momentum your book has from its five day Kindle Free promo now support a $0.99 promotion that both turns your book into the ultimate Kindle impulse purchase and leverages the many mechanisms that Amazon has for promoting your book to its 400 million plus customers.

This twin promotion strategy is exactly what I use for launching my own books and exactly what I use when launching my clients' books – and boy does it work! I've sold as many as 423 copies of one of my books in a single day using this strategy – enough for it to hit a Kindle sales rank of #247 (out of over 2 million books).

I've just finished a campaign for a client that took his book to #1 bestseller in four separate categories and to #44 in the Kindle non-fiction bestseller list – the top 100 non-fiction Kindle books on all of Amazon.

Unlike the Kindle Free promo you don't have to worry about setting anything up in your KDP account. All you have to do in terms of pricing is set your book to $0.99 before your Kindle Free promo ends. It will then automatically switch to that price ready for the start of your $0.99 promotion.

We've already covered the timing of your $0.99 promotion and how long it should run. That just leaves us with how to promote the promotion – what advertising should you put in place and how?

Promoting your $0.99 promotion

Fortunately, the steps behind promoting your $0.99 promotion are almost identical to the ones we've just gone through for your Kindle Free promo. And again, the principle is the same: you want to "prime the pump" so that Amazon will take over and start doing the heavy lifting for you – promoting your book to laser targeted buyers and generating lots of organic sales for you. The difference is that this time we are doing it for the paid bestseller lists – it's time to start getting some recognition and royalties for all the hard work you've put in!

Again, you will be best served by taking an 80/20 approach: of the many things you could be doing just focus on the few that will generate the vast majority of your results.

I've added a couple of new ideas in here. At number 7 we have running a competition or sweepstake; this is by no means essential, but if the conditions are right it can be a very cost effective way of boosting sales. At number 8 we have sending out a press release. Again, this is optional, but if it gets picked up it could have a big impact and at the very least it will have some SEO (Search Engine Optimization) value.

Here's a reminder of the other things on the list – with minor adaptations for your $0.99 promotion:
1. Discount Kindle book sites
2. Fiverr promotional gigs
3. Facebook groups
4. Facebook promoted posts
5. Twitter
6. Email your list (and any other lists you can)
7. Run a competition or sweepstake
8. Press release and contact local media

The process for setting these up is almost exactly the same as for your Kindle Free promo. As I said earlier, I recommend that of your total advertising budget you spend around a third on your Kindle Free promo and the remaining two thirds here on your $0.99 promotion.

Below are a few notes on things to be aware of when setting up your $0.99 promotion.

1. Discount Kindle book sites

The good news here is that there are now lots of sites promoting *discount* Kindle books, whereas until early 2013 the focus for most sites was on promoting *free* Kindle books. This is because of changes to the Amazon Associates Program that came into effect in March 2013, penalizing associates if they generated too many free book downloads – in fact, Amazon said they wouldn't get paid at all!

With the thresholds for free book downloads set so low (compared to the numbers being generated at the time) many sites stopped promoting free books altogether and switched to a discounted pricing model.

This has created a great opportunity for Kindle authors willing to take advantage of it. Overnight it became possible to promote discount Kindle books to tens of thousands of avid Kindle readers all hungry for bargain content. What this means is that it is no longer necessary for us to rely entirely on the momentum generated by Free Kindle promos. Now, in the space of a few days, we can sell hundreds or even thousands of discounted Kindle books – all of which count towards our paid Kindle sales rank.

As with the free book promotion sites, I look primarily for sites with a worldwide Alexa.com rank of 250,000 or less and/or a US Alexa.com rank of 100,000 or less.

Here is a non-exhaustive list of sites where you can promote discount Kindle books and which either fit those criteria (at the time of writing) or which are cheap enough to still be worth advertising on:

AskDavid.com
AwesomeGang.com
BargainBooksy.com
BargaineBookHunter.com
BookBub.com
BookGoodies.com
DailyFreeBooks.com
DigitalBookToday.com
eReaderGirl.com
eReaderLove.com
eReaderNewsToday.com
fkBooksandTips.com
IndieBookofTheDay.com
KindleBookPromos.Luckycinda.com

KindleNationDaily.com
PixelofInk.com
PixelScroll.com
TheeReaderCafe.com
TheKindleBookReview.net
VesselProject.com
WorldLiteraryCafe.com

Note that where words have been capitalized it is to make the URLs easier to read in case you need to type them – they are not case sensitive.

2. Fiverr promotional gigs

Follow the same steps as when running your Kindle Free promo.

3. Facebook groups

Follow the same steps as when running your Kindle Free promo.

4. Facebook promoted posts

Follow the same steps as when running your Kindle Free promo.

5. Twitter

Follow the same steps as when running your Kindle Free promo.

6. Email your list (and any other lists you can)

If you have a list, now is the time to email them. I recommend that you email them at least once a day while your book is on special offer – unless, of course, you plan to keep it at $0.99 for an extended period of time in which case just the first two or three days.

Make it clear how much of a bargain they're getting and also that they only have a short time to take advantage of the offer (again, assuming this is true).

A tactic that can work very well is to offer your list some sort of bonus if they buy your book on a certain day or within a certain time period. It might be a free book, a free video training or a webinar – ideally, some sort of content that can be delivered digitally so it won't cost you anything. The bonus could also be entry into a competition – see below.

And as I mentioned in Part V, if you can get anyone else to email their list on your behalf to promote your discounted book then definitely take them up on that!

7. Run a competition or sweepstake

Running a competition or sweepstake that gives people a chance to win a cool or exciting prize can be a great way to create buzz and engagement and boost your other promotional efforts. There are, however, a few things you need to consider first.

In terms of your main prize, you want to hit that sweet spot where you're offering something that's exciting enough to make people take action without being prohibitively expensive. An example of an attractive prize that won't break the bank would be a new Kindle Fire. It fits extremely well with your target market, is a cool prize and has a sufficiently high perceived value to encourage action – and yet, at the time of writing, you can buy a brand new 7" Kindle Fire HD from Amazon for just $139.

It's also a good idea to have plenty of smaller prizes as well – people love to win stuff, even if the prize is only a small one! These prizes need not be expensive at all. For example, you could send people signed copies of your book (if you have a physical version – something we'll cover in the next chapter). If you're writing in the non-fiction "how to" space you could offer something like access to a private group coaching session.

Be clear on what you want people to do

You need to be very clear to people about what they need to do to enter the competition. I recommend sending people to a landing page with clear, step-by-step instructions; screenshots to illustrate exactly what they need to do; links to your book's Amazon page; and, the email address where their entries should be sent, if applicable.

Prior to running your competition

If you have a list or social media following give people some heads up and get them excited about the chance to win the prizes. Explain why you're doing it – that you've got a big book launch coming up and that getting your book to bestseller status is a big deal. If people understand what it's all about they're more likely to support you.

What steps should you ask people to take?

Obviously, the exact steps will depend on what you want people to do, but here is a typical sequence:

1. Ask people to buy the book on a specific day from Amazon.com (whichever day you want your sales to peak) and provide them the direct link to your book's Amazon page. Make sure you tell them it will be discounted to only $0.99 and that they're getting a great deal on it.
2. Tell them to email a copy of their receipt to the competition email address.

That's it!

Don't forget to tell people how you'll be selecting the winners and what date you'll be announcing the results. To generate extra buzz you can do the draw on video – if it's live through Google Hangouts or YouTube Live that's even better!

Keeping things as simple as possible will maximize the level of engagement and that's what you want as it means more sales.

Asking for reviews

I've seen a number of people running competitions where they ask for reviews in exchange for entry to a sweepstake or raffle. In their terms of service, however, Amazon state that the only thing you can offer in exchange for a review is a review copy of your book.

To double check whether or not a raffle would be caught by this provision I contacted KDP team and unfortunately (because it works well) it is indeed against Amazon's terms of service. Now this doesn't mean you would necessarily get picked up for doing it, but if you did then there's a chance that all the reviews you collected during the competition time frame would be removed by Amazon.

Remember, if you get the launch right and it's a good book then the reviews will look after themselves.

Leverage your competition

A competition is something you can leverage to support all your other marketing efforts, with the exception of advertising on discount Kindle book sites. Being able to offer people a book discounted to $0.99 is good – being able to offer them a free chance to win a Kindle Fire HD on top of that is even better!

Comply with any relevant laws for your jurisdiction

Make sure that you comply with any relevant laws in your jurisdiction concerning competitions, sweepstakes and raffles as the case may be. Similarly, check that you're in compliance with any relevant rules on websites you are using to promote your competition.

8. Press release and contact local media

Press releases serve two purposes. The obvious one is to tell people about your book. Of course, this only really works if your press releases get picked up, in which case they can have a powerful effect.

The other purpose relates to SEO (Search Engine Optimization). Having a link back from a press release to your book's Amazon page can help it to rank well on Google – particularly if you're targeting longer tail keywords.

My favorite site for press releases is PRWeb.com. You have to pay to submit a press release, but PRWeb is taken much more seriously than most of the online press release sites out there. You'll also get more of an SEO boost.

PRWeb offer various pricing options and you need to pick one that allows you to put in a link back to your book's Amazon page. PRWeb allow you to use anchor text, which is, of course, a prerequisite for successful SEO.

To be able to include anchor text you will need to choose the "Advanced" option, currently priced at $249. Alternatively, you may want to go up to the "Premium" option at $369. It's not cheap, but it gets national media distribution via the Associated Press to various premium news outlets such as USA Today, the New York Times and the Washington Post.

The "Premium" option also allows you to embed a video – for example, a book trailer or a video of you describing the book that also serves to convey your personality. This will increase engagement and increase the likelihood of your press release getting picked up.

The stronger the story behind your book and the more topical the angle of your press release the more it will make sense to go for the "Premium" option. PRWeb have clear guidelines on their site on how to write and structure a good press release and what information needs to be submitted. You can check out the different PRWeb packages here:

service.prweb.com/pricing/compare-packages

Or use this shortened URL: **bit.ly/prwebcomp**

A cheaper alternative to PRWeb is Webwire.com, which allows you to place a basic online press release for just $30. The distribution is not as wide and the SEO boost is likely to be smaller, however, it's not a bad deal for $30 (it has other more expensive packages too). You can check out the different Webwire.com packages here:

webwire.com/OurServices.asp

Or use this shortened URL: **bit.ly/wwservices**

If you can afford to I would recommend submitting press releases to both PRWeb and Webwire. If you do this then consider submitting different press releases so that you have two different headlines and two different story angles in the mix – you never know who will pick up on what.

As you craft your press release pay particular attention to the headline. Without a fantastic attention grabbing headline your press release, however great it may be, will not get read.

Your press releases should be scheduled in advance. PRWeb review everything that is submitted and will not release anything that does not comply with their rules. I would submit your release at least a week in advance of when you will need it, just to be on the safe side. That way you have time to make corrections and resubmit if necessary. Once it's approved you can relax and it will be sent out on the release date scheduled by you.

Your press releases should go out on the day you expect your paid sales rank to peak – probably the Tuesday or the Wednesday. Don't forget that if your book hits a particular milestone such as #1 bestseller status for its category or the fiction, non-fiction or Kindle bestseller lists then you have the makings of a follow up press release at any time.

Contact local media

Local newspapers need local interest stories to fill their pages. There's a good chance that they will write about you as a local author whose book has just been published.

Getting your story run by your local press greatly increases the chances that it will get picked up more widely. You should also remember to ask for a link (preferably an anchor text link) back to your book's Amazon page from their online edition.

Journalists are busy so set this up in advance and (if possible) get the story to coincide with the day you expect your book to peak in the bestseller lists.

Part VII: Kindle Countdown

I know I've already said that I don't recommend Kindle Countdown promotions as part of your launch strategy, but it makes sense to cover them here as they fit neatly alongside the Kindle Free and the $0.99 promotions in that together they give you a trilogy of options to choose from when promoting your books.

There's very little that you need to know about Kindle Countdowns that we haven't already covered. We looked at the advantages of Kindle Countdowns and how they work at the start of chapter 6. And in Part II of this chapter I explained why I don't recommend them as part of your launch – or, to be more precise, I said that the "hybrid" option of combining a Kindle Free promo followed by a $0.99 promotion will give you the best of both worlds and, therefore, better overall results.

However, even if you never use them as part of a launch, Kindle Countdowns are a great promotional tool in their own right both for boosting your book's sales post-launch and for generating opt-ins to your list.

Remember, however, the importance of testing (Kindle Free promo vs. Kindle Countdown) if you want to ensure you get the best possible results from your promotions long-term.

Setting up your Kindle Countdown

Setting up your Kindle Countdown is very easy. Go to your KDP Bookshelf and click on the "Manage Benefits" link next to the book you want to promote (note that you will only see this link for books that are enrolled in KDP Select).

On the next page you will see a button that allows you to choose either a Kindle Countdown Deal or a Free Book Promotion. Select Kindle Countdown Deal and click the button. Then click the link next to it that says "Create a new Kindle Countdown Deal for this book".

1. Select marketplace

This will take you on to a new page where you can set up your Kindle Countdown. The first thing you must do is select your marketplace – currently, you can set up Kindle Countdowns on Amazon.com and Amazon.co.uk. Note that if you want to run a Kindle Countdown in both marketplaces you will have to set them up separately. They don't have to be run at the same time, but normally it makes sense to do so.

2. Choose when the promotion will start and end

Next you will need to enter the dates that you would like your promotion to start and finish as well as the time of day (your promotion can run anywhere from 1 hour to 7 days).

3. Select the number of price increments and starting price

You are allowed up to 5 different price increments (depending on the list price of your book) during your Kindle Countdown. With each increment the price goes up, incentivizing people to buy right away. Select the number of price increments that you want and the price you would like your promo to start at.

4. Review promotion schedule

When you've completed step 3 you'll be given the chance to review and edit your promotion schedule. Once you're happy with it click the "Add Promotion" button and your Kindle Countdown is all set up. You will be able to edit your promotion settings until 24 hours before it starts.

Promoting your Kindle Countdown

How do you promote your Kindle Countdown? Simply follow the exact same steps as set out above for the $0.99 promotion.

Congratulations, you've launched your book!

Now that you've launched your book, what can you expect? Well, as you run your launch you will see a big spike first in free downloads and then in sales as your $0.99 promotion kicks in. It's normal to get several times as many free downloads as sales, by the way, so don't be alarmed by this! Also, don't forget to take screenshots as you run your launch so that you have a record of your success.

As the advertising for your $0.99 promotion comes to an end you will, of course, see a drop off in sales. However, if you have a good book, if you've done a good job of creating your "building a bestseller" foundations and if you've run a successful launch then your book should be ranking high in its Kindle categories and should still be making good organic sales.

What next?

As time goes on your book's sales rank will inevitably drop – that happens to all books, even the biggest blockbusters with the biggest marketing budgets behind them. But if you've done things right this drop should be quite gradual (after an initial, sharper, drop when your advertising ends). A good book that has been well marketed is likely to still be making worthwhile sales several months after being launched without any additional marketing.

With all the work you've put into your book, however, my guess is that when sales eventually slowdown you'll want to do something to boost it back up the charts. And that is what we're going to cover in our final chapter.

Chapter 10:
Post-launch marketing

This chapter covers 14 different ways of marketing your book post-launch. Please don't feel that you have to do them all – though you can expect excellent results if you do! Instead, think of it as a menu you can choose from.

As with the promotion methods outlined for your book launch, I have taken an 80/20 approach. Of the many things you could do to market your book post-launch those that I have included here are the ones that I believe get you the best results and provide the best return on investment – both in terms of your time and your money.

Here are the 14 book marketing strategies that were going to cover in this chapter:

1. Write more books!
2. Bundle your books
3. Leverage other authors' books
4. Temporary price drop
5. Run another promotion
6. Build relationships
7. Facebook or blog?
8. Getting physical: CreateSpace
9. HARO: Help a Reporter Out
10. Hard copies to journalists
11. Kindle foreign rights strategy
12. Testing: the "Big 5"

Let's start with what may be the single most effective strategy for selling more books...

1. Write more books!

This is something that we covered at the end of chapter 2 when we looked at serialization as a way of increasing royalties (and at the different ways you can serialize your books) and also in chapter 4. Someone who has already bought and enjoyed one of your books is many times more likely to buy another than someone who is a non-customer. Of course, your books don't have to be related, however, you will be able to cross-promote them much more successfully if they are.

If you need to refer back to the information on serialization and cross-promoting your books it can be found in: chapter 2 under monetization method 9: serialization; and, chapter 4, Part IV, step 10 of the 10 step Writing System.

2. Bundle your books

Bundling your books is something you can do once you have a series of related books. It's a great way to create a higher priced product, while at the same time offering your customers a great deal – a true "win-win".

So, for example, if you have a three-book trilogy you might offer all three for the price of two. Just to be clear, you still continue to sell all of the books in your bundle separately as well – the bundle is simply another way that people can buy them.

The other great thing about bundling your books is that it creates another way for people on Amazon to find your work. For example, if you've got six books on Kindle that's six ways for people to find your work. But if you also bundle your books into two sets of three you now have six books plus two bundles – now there are eight ways for people to find you and you haven't had to write a word!

This is absolutely going to increase your sales just by virtue of the fact that more people will actually discover you in the first place in addition to the fact that they are effectively making a "bulk purchase" when they buy a bundle.

To bundle your books you simply combine them into a single volume. You create a new manuscript that contains all the books in that bundle with a single table of contents that covers all three volumes. To make it easier for people to navigate the bundle I recommend you change your headings settings and use Heading 1 to link through to the start of the different books and Heading 2 for chapters and so on. Once you've created your new manuscript you publish it through KDP just the way you would if you were publishing a single volume.

Something that you should do differently, however, is the cover. You want to make clear to people that they are getting a bargain so rather than using a "single" book cover use an image that makes clear to people they are getting multiple books. This could either be a box set style image or a composite image showing the covers of the original books. Including a banner or tagline telling people that they are getting a bargain – for example, "3 for 2" – is also a good idea.

It's important that in your title and description you make very clear to people what they're getting. The last thing you want is existing customers buying the bundle at a higher price and then finding they already own one or more of the books. Apart from refunds, any negative reviews that might result will not help your sales.

3. Leverage other authors' books

What if there was a way to ethically leverage other authors' books to sell more of your own? Well there is, and almost no-one does it, making it a lot easier for you to set up as you'll likely be the only person making this kind of offer.

What this essentially involves is trading recommendations with other authors who have written related books. Now you need to balance this with the need to promote your own books, if you have them, which should take priority. However, it's a great way of introducing new readers to your work.

A strategy like this is possible because of the growth of self-publishing and the increasing number of Kindle authors who have control over their own work. It would be difficult to set this up with a mainstream published author.

The strategy works because if people are interested in a particular niche or genre they are likely to buy multiple books by multiple authors. Therefore, it is not a zero-sum game: if you cross-promote another author's work you are unlikely to be cannibalizing your own sales. This is a form of "coopetition" (a portmanteau of cooperation and competition).

If you have books of your own they should still be the first thing you promote. But after that you can include a "recommended reading section" with books from other authors.

It makes sense to only approach authors whose books will be of genuine interest to your readers. Just as importantly they should be books that you've actually read and can wholeheartedly recommend. It's also important to make sure that the books you include have worthwhile long-term sales. This is a reciprocal arrangement and there's no point being promoted in a book that never gets read.

If you "rinse and repeat" this process with a number of authors in your space you will have created the chance of being found by lots of new readers. The fact that you are being recommended increases the likelihood that they will check you out – social proof is a powerful sales tool. Plus you get to build a useful free resource for your own readers and to help and build relationships with other like-minded authors – sounds like a pretty good deal!

4. Temporary price drop

This is a very quick and simple strategy that takes no planning and almost no time to set up.

Demand for Kindle books is very price elastic. This means that if your sales are flagging you can easily boost them with a temporary price drop – even if there is no associated promotional activity.

To give your book sales a quick boost you can simply drop the price to $0.99 for a day or two. The results won't be nearly as dramatic as if you ran a proper promotion, but you will get a lift in your Kindle sales rank, which will have the effect of increasing your book's visibility for a while and generating additional sales.

The only thing to be aware of is that if you are planning to run a Kindle Countdown any time soon then your book's price must remain unchanged for at least 30 days prior to the start.

5. Run another promotion

This needs no explanation – simply run another Kindle Free promo, $0.99 promotion or Kindle Countdown.

6. Build relationships

Assuming you're in this for the long-term then it's a great idea to start building relationships with other authors and experts and with your fans and followers.

Authors and experts

Let's start with other authors and experts. Connecting with like-minded people in your field is extremely rewarding in all sorts of ways. As well as giving each other encouragement and moral support it's great to be able to exchange ideas and best practices with people.

From a marketing point of view, being able to call on a network of people who have got your back and who each have their own platform of people likely to be interested in your books is very powerful. Reciprocal arrangements whereby you support one another's book launches and promotions will allow you to quickly and easily get in front of a lot of targeted people independently of, and in addition to, those you can reach through Amazon.

This will give a tremendous boost to your promotional efforts and, obviously, the bigger and more supportive your network the bigger the boost.

Fans and followers

I've already mentioned several times the importance of building your list and building a relationship with the people on that list. Your existing readers are many, many more times likely to buy your next book than anyone else so look after them!

Social media is another powerful tool for building long-term relationships with your fans and followers. Facebook and Twitter are the obvious choices, but you should consider where you target market is. Google+, LinkedIn, Pinterest and YouTube (yes, for practical purposes, YouTube is also a social network) are all great platforms to build relationships on – but only if enough people in your target market are using them.

I recommend taking the 80/20 approach to building your social media presence. Yes, you will be able to find new readers and fans on any major platform, but you're probably better off sticking to the one or two that will give you the biggest return on your investment of time.

Whichever platforms you choose, give people a reason to join your email list as well so that you have a means of contacting them independently of your social media presence. You can use LeadPages.net to set up a squeeze page that will appear under a tab on your Facebook page. Worst case scenario it may be, but if your account was shut down or suspended for any reason you would still be able to communicate with your most enthusiastic fans.

As you build your relationship with your fans and followers always be thinking "What's in it for them?" Add massive value over the long-term and then, when you ask for people's help in your next launch or promotion they're much more likely to support you in return – it's the law of reciprocity in action.

The way to do this is to regularly send good, useful and/or interesting content out to your email list or through social media. Most of this will have nothing to do with promoting your books, products or services – it should primarily be about providing value.

There is no set number or emails, posts or Tweets you should be sending. Some people email their lists on a daily basis, some so once a week and some less often. It also depends on the medium – you can send a lot more Tweets than you can emails before people will get tired of them. Just send out interesting and useful content regularly and promote only occasionally.

7. Facebook or blog?

There are some blogs that are incredibly successful – bloggers like Tim Ferriss and Seth Godin immediately spring to mind. But for every amazingly successful blogger there are millions of blogs with little or no traffic.

The reality is that building a highly successful blog usually takes *a lot* of time and effort, and even then there's no guarantee it will really take off. In other words, if you plan to start a blog with the objective of getting lots of traffic then be prepared to commit for the long-term.

Social media has a number of advantages over blogging. Let's say that your target audience hangs out on Facebook. How often are they likely to visit your blog compared to the number of times they will visit Facebook every single day?! No need to answer that question! Social media platforms are also much easier places to build relationships, because that's exactly what they are designed for.

Another advantage of Facebook is that if you have a Facebook page you can promote your posts (not something you can currently do in Facebook groups). This gives you the ability to get your post into the newsfeeds of thousands of targeted people – all of whom have the ability to like it, comment on it and share it.

Can you get the best of both worlds?

A one or two line Tweet or Facebook post might be perfect for social media, but it's not suitable content for a blog. But what if there was a way of getting the best of both worlds? I believe there is – as long as you're prepared to create content pieces (whether text, audio or video) that are significant enough to stand as blog posts in their own right.

Once you've added this content to your blog you can then distribute it through all your social media channels so that it is appearing where the eyeballs are. In many cases, people will be able to consume that content without leaving the social media site – this is good because it increases engagement. Provide Calls to Action to get new people to follow you or like your page, as the case may be. Once they do then you have a chance to get them onto your email list.

While getting people directly back to your blog might sound like a good idea the danger is that this leads to a "one and done" interaction – unless you can capture their email on their first visit, which is a tall order. Getting people to follow or like you on social media, on the other hand, is a much smaller ask and so you're likely to get a far higher take up.

And, of course, the whole time this is going on you can still be sending out those one or two line Tweets and Facebook posts that are perfect for social media!

Guest blogging

Another approach that can work well is guest blogging – provided that the blog is a sufficiently high traffic blog and the audience is a good fit with whatever you're promoting.

So those are my recommendations – leverage the reach and popularity of social media, but give people a reason to opt into your email list so that you still have a means of contacting them directly. And if you're willing to put the extra time in that's required to create more substantial content pieces then go ahead and set up a blog. By distributing your blog content through all your social media channels you can get the best of both worlds.

8. Getting physical: CreateSpace

CreateSpace.com is Amazon's platform for creating print-on-demand (POD) physical copies of your books. Currently, it's only possible to get paperbacks done through CreateSpace; however, there are other providers that will do hardbacks if you need them.

POD technology is so advanced now that it is cost effective for Amazon to produce and ship a single volume at a time. No longer is it necessary to place a bulk order for 500 or 1,000 books that will sit in boxes for months blocking up your garage!

That said, you can buy bulk copies of your book through CreateSpace, which is great for all sorts of things. If you're speaking at an event it allows you to sell copies from the back of the room. If you're attending an event you can take copies to give to people you meet – a book is the ultimate business card! Physical copies are also great for giving as gifts to clients or for posting out to prospects as part of a powerful direct mail package. Note that while a black and white printed book can cost as little as $2 or $3 the price will go up dramatically if you want to include color illustrations. With both options you get a full color cover with a choice of glossy or matt finish so you don't have to worry about that.

So, since you've already gone to the trouble of creating a Kindle book, you might as well take advantage of CreateSpace so that you have a physical version available as well. Once both versions are available Amazon will normally be able to link the two automatically (so that both versions are linked to from each other's Amazon pages). If they are not linked after 48 hours then go to the Help page of your KDP account and use the "Contact Us" button at the bottom left to contact the KDP team who will set this up for you.

The reality is that most people will still buy the (cheaper) Kindle version of your book; however, there are several advantages to having a physical version available.

The first of these is that it having both physical and Kindle versions of your book available creates a better – and more professional – first impression. Having both formats (and their prices) displayed alongside one another on your book's page also allows you to take advantage of price juxtaposition.

Price juxtaposition is when you contrast two prices so that the cheaper price appears better value for money. In order to continue to get 70% royalties for your Kindle book it must be at least 20% less than any physical version available through "any sales channel" – including those outside Amazon.

In reality, I would suggest a much larger price differential to increase the perceived value of your Kindle book (without making it so large that it lacks credibility). For example, let's say you have a book that you want to sell on Kindle for the maximum $9.99 that still allows you to collect 70% royalties. To make the Kindle version look more attractive you could price your physical version at, say, $16.99.

If your book is only available as a Kindle version for $9.99 what you're basically saying to people is "I've got a book and it's worth $9.99." Now they have a very straightforward decision to make – is it worth $9.99 to them? By introducing your physical copy into the mix what you're now saying is "I've got a book that is worth $16.99, but you can get it for $9.99 and save $7." This creates a very different decision making process that will help you sell a lot more books.

Even if relatively few people actually buy the physical version that doesn't matter: you've succeeded in raising the perceived value of both versions of the book and making the Kindle version look like a great deal, which will increase your sales.

9. HARO: Help a Reporter Out

HARO stands for Help a Reporter Out. It's a great website that's used by print, radio and television journalists to get information from expert sources. Well, having a book immediately positions you as an expert on your subject. And for as little as $19 a month you can become one of those expert sources.

The site is free to journalists and is one of the top ranked websites in the world, so while there are no guarantees, the potential if you get picked up is enormous. Who knows – you might wake up one day and find you've got an invitation to appear on national television to speak about your book!

A top tip for getting the most out of your HARO membership is to be proactive. When you set up your account you will get daily alerts telling you about opportunities that match your keywords. Given the time-critical nature of so much reporting the sooner you can respond to a journalist's enquiry the more likely you are to be the one who is featured. And once you start appearing in the media this can have a "snowball effect" as other journalists quickly find out about you.

The address for the HARO website is **helpareporter.com**

10. Hard copies to journalists

A different strategy that can also work very well is simply to go direct: Have you written a book that is special in some way that might appeal to journalists? Is it ground breaking? Is it controversial? Does it challenge the status quo? Does it have a great human interest angle? Is it highly topical? In other words, is it something they could build a good story around?

If the answer to any of those questions is "yes" then it's certainly worth considering this strategy. Because it can be very highly targeted it need not be expensive and if a journalist does pick up the story it could be huge for your sales and your positioning.

Not only will an article about your book drive sales, it will also allow you to promote both yourself and your book "As featured in…" and can provide you with jacket quotes for the book.

The first step in this strategy is to shortlist journalists who are likely to be interested in your book. Search major online newspapers and publications for journalists who write on your topic area and note down a mailing address you can use to reach them (these are usually pretty easy to find).

Then order a CreateSpace physical copy of your book from Amazon and have it shipped to them at that address as a gift (you can even have it gift-wrapped!). Anyone who uses Amazon loves to get that distinctive Amazon package through the mail, and it's a good bet that most journalists will be Amazon customers.

Include a personalized message with your gift explaining that you thought the book might be of interest to them and why as well as

how they can contact you to find out more. Keep it brief –
journalists are usually very busy people.

Then follow up after a few days. Email can work, but a real letter is
much more likely to get noticed. If you can't find an email address
on the website you can usually call up the paper's switchboard and
get it from there. Again, keep your email/letter brief – your
objective is simply to remind them of the book and why it might be
interesting to them.

Local newspapers need local interest stories to fill their pages and
this strategy can work extremely well if you are that local author
whose book has just been published. Getting your story run by your
local press greatly increases the chances of it getting picked up more
widely. It's also worth asking for an anchor text link to your book's
Amazon page from their online edition – or at the very least, for
them to put in the Amazon page URL.

11. Kindle foreign rights strategy

As I'm sure you're aware, Amazon has multiple country specific
sites in addition to the Amazon.com original and they are regularly
adding new ones. At the time of writing Amazon has the following
websites:

Amazon.com
Amazon.co.uk (UK)
Amazon.de (Germany)
Amazon.fr (France)
Amazon.es (Spain)
Amazon.it (Italy)
Amazon.co.jp (Japan)
Amazon.in (India)
Amazon.ca (Canada)
Amazon.com.br (Brazil)
Amazon.com.mx (Mexico)
Amazon.com.au (Australia)

And although the English version your book will automatically be available on all these sites it will naturally sell many more copies if it's also available in the local language. That's a massive amount of worldwide potential if you have a book that is doing well in English.

Translating your book for other markets is very simple to do and can be highly profitable. Let's imagine that you get a successful 30,000 word book translated at a cost of $600 (see below for costs). If that book is selling in its new market an equivalent price of $5 then you will be making a royalty of around $3.50 per copy, meaning that you only need to sell 172 copies to break even – everything after that is profit.

You can find remarkably inexpensive translators on the freelance websites I've already mentioned:

1. oDesk.com
2. Elance.com
3. Craigslist

Remember, if you're using Craigslist then go to "Services" and click on "write/ed/tr8" (which stands for "Write, Edit and Translate).

The cost of hiring a freelance translator varies widely, but I recommend that you look to pay around $200 to $250 per 10,000 words. To find a good translator, you can follow a similar strategy to the one I outlined earlier for finding a ghostwriter. Hire three promising looking translators and have them each translate the same 1,000 word sample text. Then find a native speaker to review the translations to see who has done the best job. I would also strongly recommend hiring someone to proofread them for you.

12. Testing: the "Big 5"

Ryan Deiss, one of the world's leading Internet marketers, talks about the difference between testing "variables that whisper vs. variables that shout." What he means is that you'll get a lot more out of testing some variables than others – it's that 80/20 Principle at work again.

When it comes to your Kindle books there are five variables that shout:

Price
Title
Sub-title
Cover
Description

It's important to only test one variable at a time, otherwise you'll never know what's made the difference. You will also need steady sales for at least a week before you test; if anything has just happened to influence your sales give them time to settle down.

When you test, you also want to test for at least seven days so you get enough data to make a meaningful comparison. Your KDP Sales Dashboard will give you the daily sales totals allowing you to compare the "before" and "after" results.

Price

If you haven't already seen it there is a detailed video explaining how to test your prices and calculate the royalty sweet spot for your books in the free Crush It with Kindle video series that accompanies this book. To get instant access to the video series go to **bit.ly/ciwkvideos**.

Title

Believe it or not, you can actually change the title (or sub-title) of a Kindle book without affecting that book's Amazon listing in any way: its Amazon page will stay the same, its reviews will remain in place and its Amazon page URL will remain intact. I was a little bit skeptical about this so I checked it with the KDP team and then tested it on one of my books – sure enough, apart from the title changing everything else remained completely the same.

This means that if you come up with a tremendous idea for a title after publishing your book you can make the change and test it (and if it doesn't work simply change back to the original).

There is a minor issue to be aware of if you do make a permanent change to your book's title. This stems from the fact that Amazon includes keywords from your book's title and sub-title in the Amazon page URL. Since the URL does not change you may find that the keywords in the URL no longer match those in your book's title (and sub-title if that also changes). However, as long as your title change is generating extra sales I wouldn't worry about this.

Sub-Title

The same things that apply to changing and testing titles also apply to sub-titles.

Cover

We've already seen what an important variable a book's cover is. The great thing about covers is that you can split test them quickly and easily using Facebook ads without having to make any changes to your book unless you find a winning design (see step 4 of chapter 7).

Description

Your carefully crafted book description should not normally be something you need to make changes to. However, there may be times when you look at it and think that, on reflection, you could do a better job. Maybe you didn't fully emphasize a key benefit or perhaps it doesn't have quite the dynamism you thought it did. Whatever the reason you can craft a new version and test to see if it gets you a boost in sales (while keeping a copy of the original in case it doesn't).

Don't over test

While testing can be a great way to improve your sales, don't over-test or you will get a diminishing return on your time. If you have a great new idea or you think something's not working as well as expected then by all means test, but know when to leave the testing alone and focus your efforts elsewhere.

13. Getting Amazon to email for you

If you update one of your Kindle books following its publication then it's actually possible to get Amazon to email everyone who has ever bought or downloaded it to let them know.

Since the update is free and people are getting a new and improved version of the book, this will generate a lot of goodwill amongst your readers. It will also increase engagement with your book by acting as a reminder to those who've not got around to reading it yet. This, in turn, will generate new opt-ins to your list (you did set that up, didn't you?!).

The catch is that Amazon will only do this if they determine that you have made a "major" revision to your book (something they are careful not to define). If the revision is only considered "minor" people will still be able to get the update, however, they won't get an email – instead the update will only appear on their "Manage Your Kindle" page, meaning that far fewer readers will be aware of it.

For this reason, if you have a number of changes to make it's a good idea to get them all done before you notify Amazon (see below). This increases the chances they will email for you. While there are no guarantees, adding a significant amount of material such as a new chapter will probably win you an email!

None of this happens automatically. You must notify the KDP support team that you have updated your book, after which it takes them up to four weeks to review the update. You submit your notification via the "Contact Us" button on the Help page of your KDP account. By providing the KDP team with clear information about exactly what changes have been made your update is likely to go through the review process faster.

14. Life beyond Kindle...

There is, of course, life in the eBook world beyond Kindle!

Although Amazon gets the lion's share of eBook sales at about 65% that still leaves 35% of the market, most of which is split between the other major retailers: Apple, Barnes & Noble, Kobo and Baker & Taylor.

The market certainly seems to be consolidating. The Sony Reader Store closed in the US and Canada on the 20th of March 2014 transitioning its titles and customer libraries across to Kobo. Then, just days later on the 31st March 2014, the Diesel eBook store also closed.

Getting your book in front of the remaining 35% of the market does, however, involve a key decision and that is whether or not you want your Kindle book to remain part of KDP Select.

What I'm going to look at first in this section are the pros and cons of staying in KDP Select or expanding your distribution beyond Amazon. Then I will review the two leading options available to you if you want to get your book on the additional major platforms.

Should you stay in KDP Select or distribute beyond Amazon?

Amazon's KDP Select terms of service state that for your book to be part of the KDP Select program it may not be available in digital form anywhere else (including your own website). Just to be clear, if your book is not enrolled in KDP Select then there are no restrictions on it being available digitally elsewhere. Nor do these restrictions apply to physical versions of your book.

The price of having your book reach a wider market, therefore, is that you must take it out of KDP Select. Fortunately, this rule is applied on a book by book basis so your other books are not caught.

The advantages of staying in KDP Select we have covered above, namely that you can run a Kindle Free promo or a Kindle Countdown every 90 days and that your book has access to the Kindle Owners Lending Library (KOLL), which can add up to a significant percentage of your royalties.

Additional Kindle promotions are a great way to boost sales, generate opt-ins for your list and to cross-promote your other books. Cross-promotions can be particularly effective if you are promoting the first book in a series or trilogy due to the follow-on sales they lead to. If you leave KDP Select then you will be limited to running promotions where you have to manually discount your price such as the $0.99 promotion.

That's a recap of the advantages that need to be weighed up against gaining access to the remaining 35% of the eBook market. The more information you have about the sort of results you can expect for your book when running a KDP Select based promo the easier it will be to make a decision. Will gaining access to an additional 35% market share outweigh the extra promotional royalties, opt-ins, cross-promotional book sales and KOLL payments that your book can generate through KDP Select?

Bear in mind also that unless you take active steps to market your book on the new platforms your sales may well not reflect their actual market share. Your book will still benefit from the "building a bestseller" foundations you have in place, but adding it to a new platform is not the same as marketing it on a new platform.

Remember that you must actively opt-out of KDP Select otherwise Amazon automatically re-enrolls your book at the end of each 90 day period. To do this, go to your KDP Bookshelf and select "Edit Book Details" for the relevant book. On the next page click on "Enrolment Details" and a pop-up window will appear. Uncheck the automatic renewal radio button in the pop-up window and then click "Save".

If you do decide to market your book more widely the decision is not set in stone. Should you find that the results do not justify leaving KDP Select then it is possible to re-enroll. However, to do this you will need to unpublish your book from the other platforms it is on. This can be done via your aggregator site (see below) – however, the process can take several weeks.

Aggregator sites: Smashwords or BookBaby?

If you decide to publish your book on the other major platforms then I strongly recommend using an aggregator site to do so. There is a cost involved but it is an efficient 80/20 approach that provides you with a one-stop shop for both distributing and updating your books.

There are several aggregator sites to choose from, but the two main players are **Smashwords.com** and **BookBaby.com**. The services they offer are similar and there is no clear-cut answer as to which is best.

To make things easier I will highlight some of the key differences but, be aware that these can change all the time. Much of the information available in online articles comparing the two sites is at least partly out-of-date even though it's often as little as a few months old. The information below is based on that found on the two services' websites and is correct at the time of writing.

Smashwords

Smashwords will distribute your book on all of the most important platforms including Apple, Barnes & Noble, Kobo and Baker & Taylor, plus a variety of smaller platforms.

There is no cost for listing your book on Smashwords – instead, you are charged 10% of the retail price of your book. This means that if your normal royalty would be 70% then, after Smashwords has taken its cut, you will receive 60%. Smashwords is also a book seller in its own right and will pay you a very generous 85% royalty on any books it sells directly.

Another nice thing about Smashwords is that you can simply upload your book as a Word file – unlike BookBaby, which requires you to either submit your book as an ePub file or choose one of their paid options (see below) and have it converted.

BookBaby

BookBaby will also distribute your book on all the most important platforms (Apple, Barnes & Noble, Kobo and Baker & Taylor) plus several smaller platforms, which differ slightly from those offered by Smashwords.

It has three distribution packages offering different combinations of upfront fees and royalty charges. If you choose their "free" package it is indeed free to list, however, you will be charged 15% of the retail price of your book and you must supply your own ePub file. If you don't have an ePub File (and don't want to outsource the file conversion) then you have a choice of the standard or premium packages. The standard package is $99, which covers the cost of converting your file to ePub. On top of this you will still be charged 15% of your book's retail price.

BookBaby's premium package looks expensive at $249, particularly compared to a free listing on Smashwords. However, if you pay for the premium package you will not be charged any royalties so if you are selling a reasonable number of books it may be the best long-term choice (see example numbers below).

There is, however, one big catch with BookBaby and that is the amount they charge if you need to make corrections to your manuscript. For "spelling or minor punctuation changes" you will be charged $50 for 1 to 10 changes – yes, this could mean it costs you $50 to fix a single typo! To make 11 to 25 changes will cost you $75 and to make 25 to 50 changes will cost $100. For more than 50 changes you will be charged $150 per hour.

This contrasts rather sharply with the ability to correct your manuscript for free on Smashwords!

On top of this BookBaby state that:

> *"Any changes beyond spelling and punctuation will necessitate a new edition of your eBook, which will require a new eBook submission, submission fee, and ISBN number."*

Again, contrast this to both Smashwords and Amazon where you can simply upload your revised manuscript for free.

It is worth noting that while you should assign a new ISBN to your book if you are making significant content changes, this is not the case for relatively minor updates. The guideline given by Smashwords is that a new ISBN is not required if "customers would consider it the same book." The US based National Book Network, meanwhile, suggest that 15 to 20% of a book's text or content should change for it to be treated as a new edition. It certainly seems to be the case that the ability (particularly on the part of self-published authors) to update eBooks so easily is blurring the lines as to when a new ISBN is needed.

The Kindle version of your book does not need an ISBN in any event (though you can choose to assign one) as Amazon automatically assigns it an ASIN.

Comparing the numbers

With a royalty charge of 15% of retail price neither the "free" or standard packages from BookBaby stack up against the 10% of retail royalty charged by Smashwords. What may make sense, however, is to choose BookBaby's royalty free premium package at $249.

Here are the numbers of books you would have to sell to break even on BookBaby's $249 listing fee compared to Smashwords 10% royalty charge based on some common book price points:

At $2.99 = 833 books
At $4.99 = 499 books
At $9.99 = 250 books

Of course, these numbers do not take into account the additional costs charged by BookBaby if any corrections are needed. And if you needed to update your book then you would be charged an additional $249 and would have to sell the same number of copies all over again to break even for a second time.

On balance

While I don't like the fact that BookBaby charges authors so much for corrections and updates, it does make sense long-term if you have a book that is making worthwhile sales, is error free and which you will not need to update.

The time during which your book is exclusive to Kindle can help you reach this point, since even when working with editors and proofreaders it's almost inevitable that a small number of typos and mistakes will slip through. As you discover these (or as readers point them out to you) they can be fixed until your book is finely tuned and mistake free.

On the other hand, for a book like this one that needs constant updates – because the Kindle publishing landscape is changing all the time – BookBaby makes no sense at all: for Crush It with Kindle Smashwords is a no-brainer.

Chapter 10 recap:

So there you are – 14 different ways of marketing your book post-launch. As I said at the beginning of the chapter: though you can do them all please don't feel that you have to. Instead, think of this chapter as a menu of ideas to choose from whenever you need them. Some you might do multiple times; some not at all.

Each of the 14 strategies has also passed the "80/20 test". In other words, each one will give you a good return on your investment of time and money (though most are free or inexpensive anyway). And they've all been tested in the field multiple times.

Most of the strategies covered are things that either you do once and forget about; do only occasionally; or, if you need to do them more than once, don't take up a lot of time. The only things on the list that (if you choose to do them) require a level of ongoing commitment are relationship building, social media and blogging. And that's the whole point! These strategies are designed to give you the biggest possible bang for your buck without taking up lots of your time. They free you up so that you can write more books, grow your business and enjoy your life.

What next?

I'd like to leave you with a few thoughts on Kindle publishing and a writer's call to action. It's easy to become blasé about all the technology we have available. In what seems like the blink of an eye we've moved from a world of desktops to a world of laptops, tablets and smart phones.

Over a similar time period, Web 2.0 has created incredible opportunities for all of us. The gatekeeper is dead. We no longer have to compete with thousands of other writers to find an agent before our work can even be seen by prospective publishers. We can now make our work available on Kindle and let the public decide if they want to read it or not.

I'll say it again – this is an incredible opportunity! We are truly privileged to be able to do this. We live in an amazing age.

You now have the information you need to write, publish, promote and monetize your Kindle books successfully. All you need to do now is take action – which is where most people fall down. You, on the other hand, have already taken action and read this book which puts you way ahead of the game. It's now time to get writing, get publishing and get promoting: nothing will change until you do.

Carpe diem

Good luck and happy writing!

John

P.S. Please see the review request on the next page! ☺

Review request

By now you know how important good reviews are to the success of a book on Kindle. You also understand why this review request is at the back of the book not the front and why it's sitting on its own page!

If you enjoyed this book or if you found it useful I'd be very grateful if you'd post an honest review. Your support really does matter and it really does make a difference. I do read all the reviews so I can get your feedback and I've made a number of changes to this current addition as a result of that feedback.

If you'd like to leave a review then all you need to do is go to the review section on the book's Amazon page: **bit.ly/ciwkbook**

You'll see a big button that says "Write a customer review" – click that and you're good to go!

Thanks again for your support.

Yours in friendship

John

Link to book's Amazon page: **bit.ly/ciwkbook**

Final reminder

This is your last chance to grab your FREE BONUS video series.

So if you haven't grabbed it already, now's the time to get instant access.

The videos feature additional bonus material that is better suited to video format. They also build on some of the key things covered in the book so watching them will allow you to get as much as you possibly can from the book.

To get instant access to the videos go to **bit.ly/ciwkvideos**

Amongst other things, the video series includes additional information on:

- Maximizing your Kindle royalties
- The 5 steps to a Kindle bestseller
- The incredible explosive growth of Kindle publishing
- Case studies and success stories

So, to get your additional bonus videos go to **bit.ly/ciwkvideos** now.

Made in the USA
Middletown, DE
19 December 2019

81311947R00141